THE PHILOSOPHY OF POLITICS

*****

The Summary Cause for the Stability or Downfall of Human Societies

ANTONIO ROSMINI

THE PHILOSOPHY OF POLITICS

Volume 1

The Summary Cause for the Stability or Downfall of Human Societies

Translated by
DENIS CLEARY
and
TERENCE WATSON

ROSMINI HOUSE
DURHAM

Rosmini House, Woodbine Road
Durham DH1 5DR, U.K.

Translated from
Della sommaria cagione per la quale stanno o rovinano le umane società
Milan, 1837

Typeset by Rosmini House, Durham
Printed by Bell & Bain Limited, Glasgow

ISBN 1 899093 00 1

Note

Square brackets [ ] indicate notes or additions by the translators.

Paragraph numbers have been added throughout the work by the translators

Foreword

This translation of Rosmini's *Philosophy of Politics* was prompted in part by the need for an English edition of works frequently quoted by the author in his *Philosophy of Right*, two volumes of which* have already been published. This need, however, must not be considered the prevalent factor in determining the immediate issue of *The Summary Cause for the Stability and Downfall of Human Societies* and *Society and Its Purpose*, which make up the *Philosophy of Politics*. Far more important is the present state of civil society, and our general understanding of the nature of society.

We live in a civilisation where photo-opportunities and sound-bites are rapidly taking the place of reasoned argument in civil affairs; we are not given the opportunity of asking about the purpose of society, nor about the nature of its essential elements, nor about the means by which society is to achieve its end. This is particularly dangerous at moments of history marked by gross materialism with its inevitable tendency to individualism. Consumerism, our own brand of materialism, is necessarily destructive of the union between persons on which society depends.

It is a simple fact that social groupings of every kind are under threat, and will not be saved from destruction without a concerted effort to re-discover the fundamental principles on which society is founded.

Rosmini's *Philosophy of Politics* provides a framework within which the discussion can be revived or initiated, and carried forward. Although written over a century and a half ago, its basic argument has not been outdated. In some ways, the thrust of the work seems more urgent than ever.

* *The Essence of Right* and *Rights of the Individual*, Durham, 1993.

When Rosmini asks, for example, what government is for, and what it has to achieve, we recognise gaps in our own questioning and understanding. How can we exercise responsibly our rights as enfranchised citizens if we are ignorant of the purpose of government? Can we vote responsibly, and thus contribute to the well-being of society, without some opinion of the progress expected by society from its elected representatives?

These and other questions are also relevant to the means by which government intends to achieve its aim after setting correct priorities for its own nation and itself. Dynamism is not everything. Looking in the right direction, but moving in the opposite way can often be more dangerous than marking time. What we need from government is the foresight to balance interests in society so that society as a whole will be able to make progress.

This progress, Rosmini maintains, is found only in the contentment realised by the spirit of the members of society. In other words, the aim of society is true, human good. This is a complex end, which does not and cannot consist in material well-being alone; it is an end which takes account of persons rather than things; it is an end in which virtue, the only source of contentment, is prized above all else; an end which has to be provided for by all particular political sciences, including economics. If this end is forgotten or ignored, only a facade of society remains. The internal will for society has vanished and the external apparatus, solid though it may appear, is doomed to perish.

The supreme, mortal error is to lose sight of the substantial reality which sustains society, and devote total attention to what is accidental. A materially privileged people, full of whinging malcontents, is not a society on the march to greater well-being, but a group in need of salvation. The big business of commercial football, to take an trivial example, may not bring the same contentment to its 'teams' as the junior school league does to its members. A more serious example of the depth of inward contentment is that of Numa Pompilius who, when 'he set up an altar to Good Faith, that is, to a code of morality, was more aware than modern economists of the meaning of economy.'

Rosmini's aim in this book is to open our eyes to the formative elements of society, to indicate the means needed for the preservation of this inner reality, and to show that neglect of these means leads to the downfall of every society. He achieves his purpose brilliantly in a profound meditation which combines great depth of thought with careful observation of history and living reality. But above all he draws attention to the fundamental principles which alone sustain both individuals and society.

DENIS CLEARY
TERENCE WATSON

Durham
July 1994

Contents

THE SUMMARY CAUSE FOR THE STABILITY OR DOWNFALL OF HUMAN SOCIETIES

Chapter

Chapter

Preface to the Political Works

CIVIL POWER and PHILOSOPHY should act in harmony for the same end; they should not be dealt with, as they are now, by people of different talents.

Plato, *Rep.* 5

(1). Philosophy, we have said,[1] is the science of ultimate reasons. Every discipline, therefore, has its own philosophy because each of them must contain the ultimate reasons to which all others are reduced. There will be a philosophy of jurisprudence, medicine, mathematics, literature, fine arts and so on. In the same way, there will be a philosophy of politics whose concept and purpose will be clarified in this Preface to works on political philosophy.

(2). Civil government has the mission of directing and leading the society over which it rules to the end for which the society has been instituted. To reach this end, politics (the greatest of all arts) must like every other art use only means which are proper to it. Civil government, which deals with the art of politics, must

(1) Cf. *Introduzione alla Filosofia*.

restrict its action to the use of means proper to this art and within governmental power.

Politics as a science, therefore, is concerned with determining the nature of civil society and its proper end. It must go on to deal with the concept of civil government, and determine both the means it possesses and the means under its control, as well as the most suitable way of using them.

(3). But if this is the business of *politics* taken in its generic sense, what is the special function of the *philosophy of politics*?

The political means which a government can and must make use of are innumerable; some are more important than others. There is also a *way* of using them to produce their effect; this, too, often depends upon calculations extending to innumerable circumstances. Special political sciences deal separately with these means: political economy, for example, studies variations in wealth, military science the armed forces, criminal science laws intended to repress crime. The same can be said about all other sciences: wealth, the armed forces, laws and so on are so many special means used by politics. But it is not sufficient that each of these means be dealt with separately; they have to be considered as a whole, their relative power measured, and their total effect on the end of *civil* society calculated.

(4). Our first thought must be to classify or generalise the countless means open to political theory. Generalising them implies seeking the common qualities which can serve as a base and foundation for the numerous, extensive classes in which these means are distributed. Here we have to be careful: such a generalisation and classification is not produced arbitrarily. We cannot choose as our foundation *any* common quality which the means may possess. The quality which helps in classifying political means must not be accidental to them nor foreign to their suitability as political means. It can only be an essential quality, that is, their aptitude and efficacy for bringing about the end which society is directed. This aptitude alone constitutes political means which, if unsuitable for acting upon civil society, would be useless in the hands of government. As we said, although political *means* taken separately are innumerable, many of them contain the same *aptitude* for action or at least the same species of aptitude. In fact, their aptitudes, which are far fewer than the means themselves taken separately, can serve as a base for reducing political means to classes determined precisely by the kinds of aptitude they have for facilitating public affairs.

(5). Moreover, these aptitudes themselves can be generalised and reduced to lesser classes in which arbitrariness has no part. The foundation of this second classification, more general than the first, depends upon finding the *reason* underlying the *aptitudes*. For example, newspapers are political means. But to which class of means do they belong? Examining their aptitude, we find that they are suitable for educating people. They belong, therefore, to the class, 'education'. This is their first classification. We could then search for a more elevated and general way of classifying them by asking *why* education is so suitable for helping the end of society.

This can only be accounted for by a study of humankind. We would have to investigate the way in which human beings are directed to a given course of action. In doing so, we would find that human actions are influenced by two sources, *cognitions* and *felt experiences*, which can come from outside us. If we know what is true, and endeavour to arouse benevolent, virtuous affections in ourselves, we will come to do what is good; if we ignore what is true, feed on falsity and put ourselves in the grip of evil, vicious passions, we will direct ourselves to evil. Consequently, the reason explaining the suitability of education as a means of assistance for government is its existence as a principle influencing human actions. As such, it can constitute the base of a broader kind of political means which can be expressed as follows: 'Means which have some influence in determining whether human beings act well or evilly.' This kind of means is infinitely more extensive than the preceding class, which could have been expressed as: 'Means of education.' Nevertheless, this class in its turn is much broader than that of newspapers, which are only one of the many channels through which knowledge can be imparted to the people.

This of course is only an example, but it is sufficient, I think, to show how political means can be reduced to certain species, and then to ever more extended genera until we reach the final few classes or even a single principle which would provide the elegance and completeness sought in every branch of science.

(6). At this point we have to retrace our steps a little. Having seen that the successive classification of political means is not arbitrary we must consider carefully the *bases* we have indicated as the foundations of different classifications. We said, the first degree of generalisation has as its base the different aptitudes of political means, that is, the qualities which make the means efficacious in assisting civil society to reach its end. This is the *reason* why it is a political means. But we rise to a greater generalisation, we said, by asking the *reason* for the aptitudes possessed by political means. Asking *why* aptitudes are what they are means seeking the reason explaining them. The reason for aptitudes, which is the reason for the means, is therefore only the reason explaining the reason of political means, in other words, a higher reason.

It is clear that by rising to a more general class of means, we move from a lesser to a greater reason: the more general classes become, the higher the reason on which they are founded. This principle leads us directly to understand that in arriving at the most extensive classes, we have by that very fact arrived at the *ultimate reasons* of political theory. If we then succeed in pushing the generalisation far enough to reduce all the classes to unity, we have inevitably found the *ultimate reason* explaining the action of political means, that is, the principle of political theory.

It is not difficult to understand now what we mean by the phrase: *philosophy of politics.*[2] We said that philosophy in general is 'systematic knowledge of the ultimate reasons for things'; the special philosophy of politics must be 'that science which seeks the ultimate reason or reasons by which political means can obtain their effects'. These final reasons for the efficacy of political means can also be called the *most general means* of political theory. As we said, they are the foundation according to which political means are classified in the most general way.

(7). Having clarified the definition of the philosophy of politics, we are now in a excellent position to deduce its function, character and natural division.

First, its *function*. Political philosophy sets out to teach the *way* in which a government can make the best use of political

(2) Another name for this teaching is *political philosophy* (just as we say *moral philosophy*) or *philosophical politics.*

means. The so-called *special political sciences* deal with these means, but only by considering them separately, without showing how the means must be used to bring about the intended complex effect. Economists, for example, will tell us how to augment private and public wealth which, however, is only one element of true social prosperity. People can be wicked and unhappy even when wealth abounds. Wealth, moreover, is quite capable of destroying itself.

We need a more elevated science than political economy; we need some kind of wisdom to guide economy itself and determine how and within what limits material wealth can be directed towards the true human good for which civil government was instituted. The same can be said about any other means: physical force, social organisations, political laws, education, and so on.

Such wisdom teaches the genuine use of these political means which it rules, apportions, balances and directs harmoniously to prevent their doing more harm than good, and to bring about the greatest possible good of which they are capable. This wisdom is derived and imbibes from the fountain provided by the *ultimate reasons* of political theory.

In fact, the ultimate reason according to which any means is of use for the end of society also judges the lesser reasons and separates within them, so to speak, the formal from the material. In other words, it separates their sap, their life, from any obstacle of a useless outer covering.

For example, it is said that promoting education is useful because an increase in common knowledge is advantageous. This is the first and natural reason to be offered. We could ask, however, why knowledge is advantageous. Our answer would have to be: 'Because through knowledge we arrive at the possession of truth.' The more truth we possess, the further we find ourselves from error and the bad effects which result from error and indeed from ignorance. Clearly this higher reason illuminates and rules the preceding reason. Realising that knowledge is good only in so far as through it we possess the truth, I am immediately aware of the kind of knowledge and education I should seek. I see immediately that some errors pass for knowledge, and that I have a responsibility for eliminating such unwarranted knowledge from society with means falling within my competence. If, for example, I am in charge of public affairs, I can no longer be content with saying or doing what is necessary to encourage everything that passes as knowledge. I have to see that all men and women are assisted in their search for true knowledge and in their attainment of truth. This is how the *ultimate reasons* in political theory, and in every other genus of things, direct the lesser, proximate reasons.

The philosophy of politics, therefore, as the science of the ultimate reasons, is also *political wisdom* placed on high to guide all political means directly to the end proposed by human beings when together they formed civil communities. Political philosophy, considered in its essence, investigates the ultimate reasons of the art of government; likewise, considered in its application, it is 'the branch of knowledge which teaches the best use of political means.'

(8). If we consider more carefully this noble function of the philosophical part of politics, we shall understand better the *character* of the science to which the works in this collection belong.

Civil government would be useless if the decisions it takes were not aimed directly at the end of the society over which it presides. This would also be the case if, while directed to their end, such decisions remained inefficacious. Government decisions, that is, the means government adopts, have therefore to be 1. well directed; 2. of their nature efficacious.

(9). Such means cannot be well-directed, however, if government is ignorant of the ultimate, complex end of civil society. We need to note that special political sciences do not and cannot ever teach us the nature of this ultimate, complex end. As we said, the object of their investigations are special means which of their nature have special ends and produce only special effects. For example, financial science teaches us to administer efficiently the income of the State, to collect taxes with the greatest economy, to distribute them equally with the least possible trouble to contributors, with the least damage to production, and so on. These are the special ends of this science, but they are not the general, complex end of the State.

Special, lesser ends exist, therefore, but the State has in addition a general, ultimate, complex end to which all others must be subordinated. Special political sciences determine special ends, and teach us how to attain them, but only the philosophy of politics will teach us to subordinate these ends to the ultimate, unique end of civil society, and genuinely determine the true end of the great association we call *civil*. Only the philosophy of politics teaches us not to fix our eyes on some intermediary, partial end, but to consider and deal with such ends simply as means towards the ultimate end. Strictly speaking, partial ends are not in fact ends, but only means.

The philosophy of politics imposes an inviolable law upon all governments which obliges them to turn all they do to *true human good*. It does this not because the end of civil society is human good in all its extension, but because it is that portion of good to which society is ordered as an inevitable part of human good. If civil society did not pertain to true, proper human good, it would not tend to good in any way; it would be formed for evil — a truly absurd proposition.

(10). Granted, therefore, that the ultimate end of civil association has been clearly determined, it clearly contains the *ultimate reason* of all political means; it alone must be the ultimate rule for judging the value of these means, and the supreme principle which teaches us how to use them.

(11). We were saying, however, that the means used by government must of their nature be *efficacious*, and provide legitimate *direction* towards the ultimate end of society. We can now consider the *ultimate reason* for their efficacy, that is, the *quality, most common* to them all, which enables them to produce in social living the good effect to which they tend.

This quality, common to all political means, consists in the action exercised on the human spirit. The divisions of politics may indeed be innumerable, but 'politics' is either an empty word or 'an art by which the *spirits* of those governed are moved towards the end of society.' All human actions spring from and return to the spirit. Arts, sciences and projects of every kind are produced by human activity, which has its hidden origin and, as it were, its home in our spirit. Moreover, this activity returns with its effects to the spirit from which it sprang. In the last analysis, the products of human activity have no other natural tendency than to satisfy human desire.

In any system, therefore, it will always be true that external things can only be *means* with which to satisfy the desire of the spirit. They are valueless if they do not penetrate to the spirit and contribute something to the satisfaction it desires. This good influence on our spirit must be the characteristic, the common quality, the ultimate reason of all political means if they are truly to be *efficacious*.

The character and nature of the philosophical part of politics, of which we are speaking, is clearly depicted in what we have said. The philosophy of politics seeks and finds the end of civil society in the very nature of human beings when it prescribes that this end can only be *true human good*. It also sets the efficacy of all political means firmly in human nature by establishing that such efficacy consists solely in the good influence by which political means satisfy the desires of human nature. As a result this philosophy teaches us to know when, which and how such means are efficacious or inefficacious.

The proper *characteristic* of political philosophy is demonstrated when it leads the rulers of nations to the hearts of individuals, whose secrets it uncovers. In this profound recess of humanity, political philosophy often indicates the emptiness of the heart's calculations and the fallaciousness of its speculations. Political philosophy leads people away from deception, and brings an as yet unknown wisdom to the book of the heart, whose seals it breaks.

(12). Political theory is indeed a single subject, but made up of two parts. The material element deals with the means individually; the formal or philosophical element co-ordinates the means towards the end. It is very rare indeed for a person to be fully cognisant with both parts.

Normally politicians and philosophers are distinct personages. There are undoubtedly some positions in life which enable those occupying them to learn one part of science; other positions which favour another part. Human beings are limited, and exhaust their energies in only one of the two parts. Unfortunately, after persuading themselves that they are thoroughly familiar with what they know only in part, they become overconfident and through their consequent errors inflict damage in proportion to their influence.

Public life is certainly more adapted to the study of special political disciplines; private life to philosophical meditation. Philosophy, as we said, joins political means with the human heart — a private, not a public place — where entry is closed to those loaded with the trappings of exterior dignities. We have to despoil ourselves of all that envelops and attracts us; we have to dismiss our courtiers, strip off our regalia and come down from our thrones. Then, naked, solitary human beings, we have to try to enter by the narrow gate and pass through the dark recesses of our secret passions, hidden calculations, unbelievable pain and stifled sobs before finally reaching what is truly virtuous and vicious in our fellow human beings. A person surrounded by the immense illusion of exterior vanity needs infinite courage, heroic virtue and a sublime, firm mind to take such a tremendous step. Oppressed day and night by business, formalities and pleasure, he will have great difficulty finding the necessary tranquillity and leisure for deep meditation.

Moreover, the philosophical reflection of which we are speaking seems too humble and obscure to elevated persons of this world whose attention is drawn by so many clamorous, splendid, external affairs which lend themselves to general calculations in which entire populations become a mere cypher, and individuals are reduced to zero.

The wise, private individual seems much more suited, therefore, to cultivate the philosophical aspect of the science of government. He is not cut off either from human nature or from his fellows by some vast ocean of ambition and artificial dignities. Without fatigue or difficulty, he questions his own nature with which he is as it were in daily contact. It would seem highly proper that in the long chain of means and ends, of causes and effects, the entire sequence should pertain to the politician except for the final link that joins political means to human beings themselves.

For the last link, the public personage should turn to the poor lodgings of the sage, and ask respectfully to hear his salutary teaching.[3]

(3) One minister of State, who was also a great philosopher, proffered a true, acute comment on the various opportunities, provided by different social positions, for coming to know one kind of thing rather than another, and for comprehending one part rather than another of the art of government. He speaks of the heads of nations as follows: 'Kings are unfortunate Stylites, condemned by providence to lead their lives perched on columns from which they can never descend. They cannot see, as we can, what is happening down here. On the other hand, their vision extends further than ours. They have a

(13). From what we have said, it is clear that the distinction between politics and the philosophy of politics is not arbitrary. The facts themselves present us with the two parts we have indicated, represented more often than not by two different personages, the public and the private individual.

In fact, this distinction between the politician and the political philosopher always appeared when civil societies attained a certain degree of culture. At first, however, political means were few, although they gradually increased as experience showed that governments were able to benefit from a greater number of situations than had been thought. At this point all political means began to be dealt with separately, as we said, and reduced to special sciences. Consequently, we had a flood of books dedicated to business, industry, arts, legislation, war, relationships between States, and many similar subjects. As a result, the special sciences grew immensely, and drew far more attention than the philosophical part of politics. This, in turn, was rendered much more difficult by its need to rule and direct harmoniously with simple principles such a vast mass of political means — all of which seemed to require the entire application of one person. We should not be surprised, therefore, if we find the best axioms of political philosophy in ancient authors but, in our own days, an immense wealth of cognitions built up around the special political sciences.

(14). We have to consider that the public individual was at first only a private person who undertook public duties. Consequently, the art of politics must at first have been principally concerned with the private study of human nature rather than the political expedients which gradually resulted from experience. Politics must have been more formal than material, more philosophical than administrative. Indeed, we see that the art of politics sprang from philosophy. Seneca notes that Seleucus and Charondas learned neither in the forum nor in the waiting rooms of the juris consults the rights and laws they dictated when Sicily and Magna Grecia flourished; their education was gained in the silent, sacred recesses of Pythagoras.[4] Plato, in

certain interior tact, a certain instinct, which serves them as a better guide than the advice of those around them.

(4) *Ep.* 90.

declaring that philosophers were the best possible administrators of any State,[5] not only showed how much respect he had for the philosophical side of politics, but also indicated what was supremely good for his time. This was clearly understood by the good sense of all.

Nor should we be astonished if we see that the first political means, which the ancients considered the most efficacious, were those which exercised the greatest and most immediate effect upon human beings. Here religion was foremost. The Egyptians, who were called the founders of all branches of science, tempered everything with religion.[6] The same is true of the Persians, another school from which the Greeks learned. Take, for instance, the way in which the Persians made philosophy the governing principle in the education of the king's son, the heir to the throne. When he attained his fourteenth year, four of the wisest and most outstanding officers of State were chosen to educate him. The first had to impart religious instruction and with it, as though they were a single subject, instruction in the art of government; the second simply had to watch over him to see that he always spoke the truth; the third taught him to control his desires; and the fourth showed him how to overcome base fear by developing courage and self-confidence.[7]

All this is philosophy, pure and simple.Zoroaster's laws also, in so far as we know them, contained only religious and moral precepts.[8] Xenophon tells us that Persian legislation was especially notable because it aimed not only at punishing crime, but also and chiefly at inculcating in all hearts a horror for vice, and a love of virtue for its own sake.[9]

The same philosophical spirit is apparent in the Greek legislators. The famous laws of Crete, Athens, Sparta, Locri and

(5) *Rep.*, 5.

(6) Macrob., *Saturn.* 19. It has been noted that only three sentiments permeate and dominate the Egyptian monuments that have come down to us: 1. respect for the supreme Being; 2. respect for the king as the image of the supreme Being; 3. respect for the souls of the dead. A visit to any museum of Egyptian antiquities will provide ample proof of this observation.

(7) Xenoph., *Cyrop.* I, 2, and Plat., *Alcib.* 1.

(8) Cf. Hyde, *De Religione veterum Persarum*, Oxford, 1700, where a Latin version of the *Sad-der* can be found.

(9) *Cyrop.* 1.

Catania were partly forged from the example of known peoples and partly deducted as simple corollaries by the sages from their study of human nature. The fine arts, gymnastics, public education and similar matters tended directly to the formation of the human spirit. Religion was mixed with everything; the will of the gods was always consulted — it was not coincidental that the council of the Amphizionic League, the force unifying the whole of Greece, was situated at Delphi near the oracle.[10]

The whole art of government, therefore, started from human beings themselves and soon returned to them. It was the Romans who amplified the circle of politics. Totally alien to the humanities at first, devoted to action alone but with sound, wise judgment, they discovered through experience many still unknown political provisions. Vico makes an acute comment about the matter when he says that *wisdom* prevailed amongst the Greeks and *jurisprudence* amongst the Romans. By this, he means that the Greeks studied and wrote about the principles behind the laws (*leges legum*) while the Romans, who had presupposed and preserved these principles hidden in their spirit, wrote solely about their application and consequences, that is, they enunciated particular laws.[11]

(15). Nevertheless, a comparison between Roman and modern political ways and means shows that the former, although smaller in number and less distinct, were at the same time more complex and more philosophical. It is enough, for example, to note that the Romans knew how to make servitude pleasing and subjection glorious;[12] their great aim was not to rule a person externally, but to govern the whole person. I am not sure whether this was the result of good fortune on the Romans' part, or of their natural common sense. Certainly both aspects

(10) Nevertheless, I think Mengotti exaggerates when he maintains that the oracle itself was the work of Greek politics. Politics never went so far as to found oracles; advantage was taken of popular opinions and beliefs. The Delphic oracle sprang from superstition, not from politics. The documents used by Mengotti in his dissertation prove no more than this.

(11) *De universi juris uno principio*, etc., p. 2 ss.

(12) The maxim practised in Rome's most flourishing period is found in Livy who reports part of a speech before the Senate by Camillus' grandson in favour of the Latins, whom he had completely defeated: '"Rule" means that those who obey are glad to do so.'

were guided by a superior providence which saw to it that the first two kings of Rome represented the two elements of politics which we are trying to distinguish in these pages. The first king acted as a politician, the second as a philosopher.[13]

The choice of Numa, a foreigner,[14] whose natural love of tranquillity had always kept him clear of Rome, is indeed a fact of the greatest importance in Roman history. We see a rough, warlike people turn to a peaceful philosopher for government at the death of Romulus, the bellicose leader who had brought them together. Numa himself was astonished, and refused the throne. As he said, in proffering his excuses, he was made for peace, and devoted himself to his studies and religion, all of which were part of a person's private life; a throne and command of the fierce Roman people were different matters altogether. But the necessity for philosophy in civil governments and the usefulness of private virtues in the formation of a ruler were clearly underlined by Numa's father and Marius, his kinsman, when they persuaded him to accept the sceptre:

> Real government provides an ample field for the sage to show good, magnanimous activity. Here is his opportunity to serve the gods and gently infuse religious feelings in people. Subjects, in fact, easily conform to the example shown by their ruler. — A ferocious people is able to learn meekness and, already loaded with triumphs and spoils, come to love a just, gentle head who knows how to establish attractive laws and mild rule. And (who knows?) perhaps such a ruler will be able, without extinguishing this warlike Roman temperament, at least turn it to good by uniting cities and nations in the bond of friendship.[15]

(13) 'There were then two kings,' says Livy, 'who helped to develop the city, the first through war, the second peacefully. — The city was thus strengthened and tempered by the arts of war and peace.'

(14) From Cures, a Sabine city.

(15) Plut. in *Num.* It was Numa Pompilius who so profoundly impressed on the Romans the religious character which they never afterwards lost and of which Cicero wrote: 'We may indeed love ourselves exaggeratedly. Nevertheless, although fewer indeed than the Spaniards, weaker than the Gauls, less cunning than the Phoenicians, cruder than the Greeks, we have overcome all peoples and nations by our realisation that all things are ruled and governed by piety and religion and by that wisdom alone which springs from the divinity of the immortal gods' (*De harus.* resp. n. 19). We add the comment

These words transmitted by Plutarch are suggestions dependent upon calm, detached philosophy, and show that the two parts of government we have distinguished, that is, *politics* in its ordinary meaning and *the philosophy of politics*, correspond to a factual distinction present in the history of knowledge and government. We see these two parts cultivated at different times and by different personages; we see that they have greatly different characteristics: public life aids politics, while the philosophy of politics seeks the meditative silence of private life. Nevertheless, each helps the other. Plato, who was thoroughly conscious of the distinction between them, had every reason to desire that the two should be united in the same personages.[16]

(16). After defining political philosophy and describing its nature it will not be difficult for us to discover its principal parts if we wish to do so. We have called it the science of the ultimate political reasons, and said that its function is to apply these reasons to the special means proper to the art of government. We showed that these special means must be well directed and efficacious. The application of the ultimate political reasons, therefore, has two aims: knowledge of the value or the *efficacy* of political means, and knowledge of the best *way* to use them.

We can easily see now that the philosophy of politics must have two principal parts. The first is directed to searching for the ultimate political reasons and, above all, for the very last reason of all, that is, the supreme principle of this science. We have called these ultimate political reasons *political criteria* because they are indeed criteria which we can use to judge the value of political means and of the way of using them.

The second part deals with the application to the means of the political criteria. This leads us to know the *value* of these means and the best possible *way* of using them.

(17). We can now indicate the general subdivisions of the first part in the following schema:

of an economist: 'When Numa Pompilius set up an altar to Good Faith, that is, a code of morality, he was more aware than modern economists of the meaning of economy' (Melchiorre Gioia, *N. Prospetto delle Scienze Economiche*, tom. 1, p. 286).

(16) *Rep.*, 5.

SCHEMA

OF THE

PHILOSOPHY OF POLITICS

Part 1. Political criteria.

A. Political criteria deduced from the *end* of civil society (the supreme principle of this science is found here).

B. Political criteria deduced from the *natural construction* of civil society.

C. Political criteria deduced from the nature of the *forces* that move civil society.

D. Political criteria deduced from the *laws* which civil society follows constantly in its movement.

Part 2. Application of the political criteria to the special means pertaining to civil government.

A. Measure of the relative value of political means.

B. The way of using political means in order to obtain the end of civil society.

The Summary Cause for the Stability or Downfall of Human Societies

CHAPTER 1

The first political criterion

1. In every society there must be an element through which the society *exists* and another element through which it *develops* and perfects itself.

Clearly a society which comes to lack its essential support must inevitably collapse, like a building whose foundations have been removed. On the other hand, if the support is solid the society must endure, even when deprived of its accessories and of all its accidental embellishments.

This truth is simple and evident; it needs no proof. It will always be true that whatever particular causes we assign to the downfall of a society, the society finally perished because it had lost the energy which sustained it; if the energy had endured, the society would never have foundered.

2. The energy or force, whatever it may be, by which a society exists can be lost through two causes:

1. By an unavoidable, aggressive onslaught from outside. When this happens, as in conquests, the society is immediately laid low by violence.

2. By some internal weakness or, to use an expression of Dante, 'through defective support'. This happens when the energy by which the society exists gradually declines, and the society, because it fails to remedy the decline, eventually ceases to exist.

The first case depends upon the real positions and relationships of different co-existent societies. It forms the subject of teaching founded upon historical events and the factual state of the human race, but cannot be the object of pure theory. In this short work, I can only consider the second case and try to identify 'the summary cause for the stability and downfall of human societies'.

3. By 'summary cause' I mean that cause to which all others are reduced and in which lesser causes are included as parts in

their whole. In other words, I mean the complex or *sum* of all the partial causes united in the production of a total effect. This total effect, although resulting from the action of many conspiring forces, is one and simple and therefore, offers a correct reason for considering its composite cause as unique. I call the cause 'summary' precisely because it is made up of all that influences the production of the effect. And, as we said, this unique effect in our present discussion is the *subsistence* or *destruction* of a society.

Hence, if we demonstrate that in every society there is necessarily an element through which it *subsists* and another element through which it *develops* and embellishes itself, it will be easy to conclude 1. that the summary cause by which a society subsists is the preservation of that principle, whatever it is, which makes a society subsist, and 2. that the summary cause by which a society perishes is the destruction of this principle.

4. All this is clear. However, we can further persuade ourselves of the inconfusible disparity between these two principles of existence and of embellishment or refinement of a society, if we carefully consider that the difference between a thing's accidental refinement and its existence, substance or nature is not confined solely to societies but is truly a fundamental law. All real,[1] contingent beings known to us are made according to this law; in all of them we distinguish a substantial and an *accidental* element. Such a distinction, therefore, is very firmly grounded in both the nature and, as it were, the intimate composition of beings.

5. Moreover, if the distinction between that which constitutes the subsistence of beings and that which forms their refinement (something accessory to their subsistence) is, so to speak, the foundation or pattern of all the *natural beings* known to us, it necessarily follows that this distinction is also present in *artificial beings*, which are simply composite products produced by humans from natural beings. These composites include societies which human beings form positively among themselves.[2] Hence

[1] I say 'real' in order to exclude *ideal* beings, particularly *abstract* beings.

[2] We are not speaking about *domestic society*, which is the work of nature, but about all factitious societies. In any case, domestic society is subject to the same very general law.

we must not be surprised if in *societies*, as in *nature*, we must differentiate that which constitutes the society in its being from that which adds to it accidental perfection.

6. With this established, we can immediately determine the *first* of all rules of good government, that is, the *first criterion* for evaluating the means for governing any society whatever. This first rule and criterion is indubitably the following: *That which constitutes the existence or substance of a society is to be preserved and strengthened, even at the cost of having to neglect that which forms its accidental refinement*.

When this self-evident rule is applied to civil society, it becomes the first norm of sound politics.

In the same way we can also deduce the greatest errors in government. They are *those by which the government of a society loses sight of all that constitutes the subsistence of the society because of its excessive concern for the society's progress towards accidental perfection*.

CHAPTER 2

The universality and logical necessity of the first criterion

7. Here I must make an observation. From what has been said, it is clear that anyone who errs in politics, must first err in logic. To attribute greater value to the accidental ornaments of a society than to its subsistence is a logical error and false calculation.

Let us extend the observation further. All mistakes in practical human conduct, whether in private or public, or in political or moral matters, are always preceded by errors in human understanding, which, although often willed, remain errors of understanding. They are not willed of course in the effect they produce but in themselves. Thus, in the case we have considered, it is certain that no government intends to destroy the society it is governing. Nevertheless, while wishing to improve and perfect the society, a government can ruin it completely or almost completely. And the sole cause is a mental error, because the government does not justly calculate the overall effect of the provisions it decides to adopt for the good of the society it is governing.

This demonstrates once again the universality of the rule we have mentioned. When we apply it to government, we are simply applying a much wider rule pertaining to universal logic.

8. In fact every error of logic can be reduced to a very simple formula: 'To attribute to a subject what is accidental as though it were essential', or: 'To reason from the supposition that what is essential to a subject is only accidental.' Let us examine any sophism: for example, the popular one which claims to prove that we can satisfy our thirst by eating salted meat. This says: 'Salted meat makes us drink. But drinking satisfies our thirst. Therefore salted meat satisfies our thirst.'[3] Clearly the error lies

[3] A contemporary economist presented this very argument about salted

entirely in making our need for drink an essential property of salted meat. However of the only thing essential to salted meat is its production of thirst; drinking follows simply as an accidental, not a necessary consequence of thirst. Anyone who eats salted meat and has nothing to drink certainly suffers thirst; this would not be so if salted meat truly satisfied thirst.

9. This opinion, which reduces all logical errors, speculative and practical, to a single formula, is not mine; the ancient logicians seem to have reduced every kind of sophism to it.

St. Thomas himself, following the greatest ancient writer on logic, reduces every error to this sole mistake of considering the accidents as the substance.[4] A multiple question is reduced to its minimum terms; an excellent solution, in my opinion, to the complicated problem of finding the single thread leading us out of the labyrinth of infinite errors to which human reasonings are subject. Using this simple truth, St. Thomas divides the whole mass of knowledge, or better all that can be contained in the human mind, into two great classes, both of infinite extension, according to the two kinds of objects possible to human thought. The first class includes that which is truly cognition and merits the title *knowledge*. The second class is called *sophistry* and includes the whole series of possible mental errors and illusions. In the second case the mind, when reasoning about something, neglects to consider the *essence* of the thing and confines itself to what is *accidental*; it then uses the very vague and imperfect ideas it draws from this consideration to judge and reason about the thing as a whole.

10. Enlarging on the concept of this great thinker, we see that the only things presented to us in the entire universe are composed of *substance* and *accidents*; or, to state it more generally, all things, whatever their kind and mode of being, are presented to our intellect divided into two classes. Some appear to us as existing *per se*, so that they do not need other things in order to

meat when he wrote: 'If fashion induces a woman to sell, it induces a man to work in order to buy what the woman is selling. But an increase in work equals a decrease in corruption. Therefore fashion, which induces a woman to sell, diminishes corruption.' Cf. *Esame delle opinioni di M. Gioia in favor della moda* in *Opuscoli Filosofici*, Milano, 1828, vol. 2, f. 107 ss.

[4] *S.T.*, I, q. 18, art. 1, ad 2; I-II, q. 7, art. 2, ad 2.

be conceived as subsistent. Some however are presented to us as things not endowed with their own existence, that is, they are presented as things subsisting by means of and in other things, as colours, for example, which subsist through bodies and seem to adhere to bodies. The two classes can be confused by our mind which may forget beings that exist *per se* and rest solely in those which exist *per accidens*, (that is, exist in others and through others, without being necessary to them, so that beings which exist *per accidens* can disappear without the disappearance of the being to which they are joined — colours, for example, can disappear from bodies without the bodies disappearing). When we are confused in this way, our mind is deluded and forms a sophism. Because this mental error, which results from neglect to note carefully the relationship between what is *accidental* and what is *substantial*, attributes a stable existence to only a precarious, accidental existence, our spirit also is deceived and misled, and in preference to something permanent and stable readily loves a momentary, unstable thing, unworthy of love. Consequently, reason endowed with *knowledge* or cognition of a being *per se* is a certain and faithful guide, whatever a human being undertakes to do or direct. It brings to a successful conclusion whatever has been undertaken. On the other hand, when reason is deluded by *sophistry* and follows accidents instead of the substances of things, it proves an unfaithful guide. In this case everything eventually perishes, whatever enthusiasm and apparent hope has been engendered.

11. This fact, I say, was observed by others and frequently suggested by people of good sense, although they did not reduce it to a theory. There is no better or truer description of a prudent human being than that found in the words of our outstanding writer, Daniello Bartoli, when he praised the wisdom and insight of Jacopo Lainez:

> When he attended to business and sought a satisfactory outcome and balance, his grasp of the total complex mass and confused body of elements was greatly admired. He unravelled it, dissected it and divided it up into parts, and then simply discarded as an encumbrance all that was unnecessary. He could foresee and distinguish consequences and how, as effects, they would of themselves need no attention because they are naturally present in their

> cause. In this way he restricted what was *purely substantial*, that is, the business in its entirety, to the greatest immediate truth and clarity, as happens when large proportional numbers are reduced to their lowest terms.[5]

12. This same natural logic continuously moves nations to look for substantial, not accidental qualities in their rulers. Montaigne, a perceptive author, writes:

> To praise those things in a human being which do not become his ministry or should not be his principal qualities is to deride and harm him. For example, a person who wishes to praise a prince says that he is a good painter or architect, or a good archer. The only honour given him by such praise is when it serves as an embellishment to the praise proper to him, that is, to justice or the art of governing his people in peace and in war. In this way agriculture honours Cyrus; eloquence and knowledge of the arts honour Charlemagne. Demosthenes, on hearing that Philip was praised for his beauty, eloquence and capacity for drink, replied: 'Such praise certainly becomes a woman, an advocate and a sponge, but not a king.'[6]

13. The rule, therefore, that we have laid down about substance and accidents, is confirmed by common sense. And just as neglect of this rule in the government of human societies is the summary cause of their destruction, so, considered speculatively and in general, the rule is also the summary cause of all errors of human understanding, of which political errors are only particular, practical consequences.

If we act upon a speculative error, our action will certainly be defective and produce more or less guilty and harmful effects, dependent on the circumstances and the order of the things to which our action pertains. Whatever the order of things, the effect will always be pernicious and harm that particular order. Let us apply the same logical principle to the fine arts.

In this application our principle becomes one of the most important, if not the first tenet of aesthetics. It offers us perhaps the safest of all possible criteria for judging good taste in the arts.

14. In fact, we are able to see how, in works of art, any

[5] *Dell' Italia*, bk. 4, c. 15.

[6] *Essais*, bk. 1, c. 39.

superfluous embellishment or decoration not required by the intimate nature of the thing in question is defective, overdone and distasteful. We see that the decoration does not derive as a necessary consequence from the thing's nature; it is simply a false embellishment, not applied to help us understand the beauty of the whole and the perfection of the substance of the work itself. An infallible symptom of the decadence of the arts is present when artists begin to lose sight of the connection between exterior ornament and the interior structure of the work. Once this connection is lost sight of, there is no longer any limit to the multiplication of ornament. This explains the heavy, baroque taste of the 17th. century: artists lost sight of the whole, of the totality, and of what is substantial to the work, and concerned themselves solely with accessory, accidental parts.

15. The principle, therefore, which we have given as the summary cause for the stability and downfall of societies, as the first rule for their government and as the first criterion for evaluating political means, is a universal principle. It is one of those principles seen as true in all cases, which dominate and regulate without exception all orders of things whether ideal, or practical and effective.

CHAPTER 3

The first political criterion is confirmed by history — The period of the founders of societies — The period of the legislators

16. The universal, summary cause of the stability and downfall of societies, which we have found to lie in their intimate nature, will act as a key for revealing the secrets of history as it narrates the birth, growth and decline of the greatest human societies or civil states, and of their devastating changes.

17. First, it is certain that at the beginning of all societies, especially political societies, founders can neither lose sight of what sustains such societies, nor therefore neglect the rule we have put forward. It is impossible to attend to embellishments when all thought must be directed to bringing a society into existence. Moreover, while the society grows and flourishes, the principles on which it was founded and from which it drew its being are uppermost in the minds of all.

18. Consequently, it was clearly nature itself and necessity, not speculation, that taught the founders of long-lasting societies the rule already described of attending directly to the substance of society. The most celebrated legislations consisted solely in accepting and committing to paper the foundations on which the first leaders had built their societies. This explains why the oldest legislations appeared so sound and became so famous.

19. Let us limit ourselves to the constitutions and political maxims of the Spartans and Romans, the best known of the ancient world. We immediately see in them the solid and, as it were, robust character to be shown in a political order where everything is directed to giving existence to a society and to strengthening it, rather than to accidental, minute embellishments.

Indeed, the intention of ancient social legislators was to concentrate, so to speak, all their citizens' attention on the substantial good of the commonweal, for the sake of which they sacrificed many accidental advantages. These advantages would certainly have increased the citizens' common prosperity and social pleasures in some way, but would also have undermined their spirit and weakened that virile quality which was the state's defence and best protection. The legislators saw in this quality, as in a strong seed ready for growth, the very existence of all the prosperity, growth, duration and glory of the commonweal. The military condition in which Lycurgus' laws placed the Spartans, and the severity and the stern simplicity which deprived them of so many pleasures, was simply an initial application of the rule we have proposed.[7] Its difficulties were fully compensated by a healthy bodily constitution, a strong, contented spirit and unconquerable union, which lasted as long as these laws endured.

20. We see the same among the Romans. They neglected both trade and manufacture (modern nations, however, for reasons I will explain later, apply themselves with great urgency to these activities, which they consider as one of the principal sources of their greatness) for the sake of agriculture and military prowess which were the almost exclusive concern of a people destined to rule the whole world. They had a defiant disregard for luxury and for every pursuit they considered frivolous. All these practices and other rules proceeded from a unique principle which they necessarily and constantly followed, enlightened by an upright nature and uncorrupted mind. This maxim shines out in their political laws, in their mode of life, in their manner of government and in their warfare. At the height of the republic, the Romans never allowed themselves to be distracted and diverted by deceptive accidentals; they consistently turned to what they saw as the *substance of things*. No war was undertaken unnecessarily; on the other hand, no peace was concluded that contained the seeds of war and could be the cause of a sudden outbreak of hostilities. On the contrary, they prosecuted war with indomitable constancy, even in extreme danger, rather

[7] The robust lifestyle of the Lacedemonians, directed entirely to preserving the substance of the commonweal while neglecting everything accidental, is apparent not only in their laws but in all their habits of life. Plutarch, in his life of Lycurgus, notes this even in their manual skills: 'Craftsmen did not work at useless things but applied their great skill to what was necessary.'

than have an insecure and dishonourable peace, which would have set them back and caused them to lose the deep consciousness they had of their own good fortune. Virgil describes this core-characteristic of the Romans in the following memorable lines, which suit our purpose exactly:

> Some will smoother beat the curving bronze:
> Others from marble living faces draw.
> Cases at law are better fought,
> Heavenly movements and rising stars
> more fittingly described.
> But you, my Roman friend, remember
> that you rule the nations by decree,
> impose your peace as norm,
> spare your subjects
> and put down the proud.
> These are your skills.[8]

Tacitus says the same more briefly, and so aptly: 'Among the Romans it is the power to rule that matters; profitless things are ignored.'[9]

According to Virgil, the grave exhortation which Anchises gives as father to his descendants was simply the maxim always given by such great men in every undertaking: Leave to other nations all the glory of the accidental ornaments of societies, but remain united in your attention to the substance of government, in conquering those who have attacked you, in being loved by those you have conquered. This exhortation, which Tacitus calls 'the power to rule' VIS IMPERII, is expressed precisely in M. Curius' reply to the Samnites who were trying to corrupt him with money: 'For me, it is not the possession of gold which is admirable, but authority over those who have gold.'[10] These clear thinkers did not stop at the *means* but went on to consider the *end* of their society; they were able to make even great sacrifices so as not to weaken the State or reduce its consistency.

[8] *Aeneid.*, 6: 845-854.

[9] *Annal.*, bk. 15, c. 31.

[10] Cicero, *De Senectute*, 16: *Curio, ad focum sedenti, magnum auri pondus Samnites cum attulissent, repudiati ab eo sunt. Non enim aurum habere, praeclarum sibi videri dixit; sed iis, qui haberent aurum, imperare.*

CHAPTER 4

Continuation: the first political criterion applied to the two fundamental laws governing civil society: the law governing *ownership* and the law governing *marriage*

21. The examples given above belong to an era when the constitutions of nations had already been written (at least in part, for they were never entirely written), and to the outstanding period of political societies when *legislators* appeared.

22. But we need to go further back in time, to a period of *darkness* which, it would seem, lacked splendour. This moment preceded the *outstanding* period, and is the time when nations *did* what the legislators afterwards *said*: What had to be done was first shown in act and later turned into law. It is this period, not that of the *legislators*, which marks social origins; it is the period of the *founders*, when the rule we have formulated is not a theory in the minds of thinkers, but an inevitable necessity confronting those who elaborate and lay the foundations of communal living, that is, of political societies.

23. We need to study this first period carefully. If we go back in imagination to the primitive state of human affairs, we easily see how nature suggests to those who wished to associate and preserve their association that they 'concentrate on matters involving the existence of their association, and neglect its accidental refinement'.

To illustrate this, I will give only two examples. They are drawn from the two great laws which, as necessary conditions of human community, had first to be present in the foundations of communal living,[11] at least from the time it began to extend. The two laws are *those governing ownership* and *marriages*.

[11] This does not mean that there was a time when society did not exist. Family society existed at the beginning, but not civil society. The laws of ownership and of marriages however were also present in family society, and indeed were its foundation. But this is history. 'Communal living' therefore

24. I. Godwin, following Morelly and others[12] who took the new theory of human rights to its ultimate consequences, proposed a system of absolute equality, even in the case of possessions. The Sansimonians themselves recently came to the same conclusion. This equality is, at first sight, surprising and seductive:

> The direct fruits of the law of ownership are a spirit of oppression, servitude and fraud. These dispositions are all equally contrary to progress in the perfection of intelligence, and generate other vices, such as greed, malice and revenge. In a society where everybody lived in abundance and shared equally in the benefits of nature, such perverse sentiments would inevitably be suppressed, and the narrow principle of egoism disappear. No one would be reduced to guarding anxiously their smallest possession, or worrying about their needs. Everybody would be ready to forget their individual interest in order to concern themselves solely with the common interest. There would be no enmity, because every cause of dispute would have been removed. Human love would regain that ascendancy which reason assigns it; the human spirit, relieved from care of the body, would be free to rise to the noblest thoughts, and in this way follow its natural habits. Everyone would be eager to help his neighbours.

25. Such imaginary happiness enchants, and finds no obstacle in our phantasy where it is completely simple and exists entirely in isolation. Trouble arises as soon as we consider it in practice, where it is necessarily surrounded by other heterogeneous objects and many circumstances, all demanding their place. This kind of happiness, considered in the midst of all these factual circumstances, becomes an impossible chimera. I need indicate only one of these circumstances and facts present in nature which render inexecutable the vague design to exclude private ownership. The fact is the natural law according to which every population grows. The human race increases naturally by geometrical progression, whereas subsistences, the produce of the earth, can increase only by arithmetical progression. However,

is concerned with the pure theory of society.

12 Prior to these, Campanella in Italy had proposed a similar concept in his political novel, *La Città del Sole*.

even this progression cannot continue, as that of population does. A point must be reached, after which the earth no longer increases its produce, although the human race's faculty for multiplication never ends. The author of the *Saggio sulla Popolazione*[13] has, in my opinion, performed an excellent service by indicating a very obvious truth whose consequences, however, easily escape us.

26. He argues as follows:

> In a free and happy state, such as Mr. Godwin has described, where nearly all the obstacles to the growth of the population would have been removed,[14] the population would grow with the greatest rapidity. If it doubles within 15 years on the American plains, it would double even more rapidly in Mr. Godwin's ideal society. But to ensure that we do not exceed real limits, let us imagine that the population doubles only after 25 years, which is slower than takes place in the United States of America. Let us also suppose, that in place of the daily half-hour's work determined by Mr. Godwin's calculations, a half-day's work is done. If we apply this to England, anyone who knows the soil, the fertility of cultivated land and the infertility of uncultivated ground would find it difficult to believe that production would double in 25 years.[15] All we could do is turn the pasture into crops and be satisfied with vegetable nourishment.[16] This system would be self-destructive because, besides inevitable illness in people nourished with relatively unsubstantial food, the land would lose the nutriments so necessary to English soil. Nevertheless, let us suppose that production doubles after 25 years. At the end of the first period, the doubled amount

13 Bk. 3, c. 1.

14 The principal obstacles to the growth of population are two: 1. the absence of the means of subsistence in the poor classes; 2. the fear of sharing their patrimony in the rich classes. In Godwin's hypothesis both these obstacles would be removed.

15 Out of the 32,342,400 acres of land in England, it is calculated that 25,632,000 are cultivated, leaving 7,710,400 uncultivated, that is, little more than a fifth of the total land. But a half of this uncultivated land is completely sterile, so that the uncultivated ground capable of production is about a tenth of the whole.

16 Pasture is about a third more than the land under cultivation. Cultivated land and gardens cover 10,252,100 acres; pasture, 15,379,200 acres.

of foodstuffs would still be sufficient to nourish the doubled population of 22 millions. But in the second period, how could the population of 44 millions be maintained, even if we suppose (and it is very difficult to believe) that in this period the same improvements were made, and the land had been broken in and made productive, resulting in a tripling of the previous produce? The quantity produced, hardly sufficient to feed 33 millions, would result in each of the 44 million individuals receiving a quarter less food. After 50 years the delightful picture of bliss colourfully portrayed by Mr. Godwin has indeed changed! Wretchedness suffocates the spirit of benevolence exercised so liberally during the time of abundance; base passions reappear; instinct, which oversees the preservation of every individual, exhausts the noblest movements of the spirit; temptations are irresistible; the crops lose their grain before it is ripe; everyone tries to provide for himself so as not to lack what is necessary, and every vice is practised together with deception, falsehood and theft. Mothers of large families lack milk; starving children search for bread; once rosy faces become pallid with misery. Benevolence vainly tries to help, but self-love and personal interest suppress every other principle, exercising an absolute dominion everywhere. If we are not convinced of what can happen in these first 50 years, the third period will have a population of 44 million people entirely without food, and in the fourth period (which would never come) 132 million will die of starvation; universal need would cause universal thieving.

27. We see here the source of the universal laws which have always governed society: their sanction is absolute necessity. Let us imagine that they have been abolished, and private ownership removed. The rapidly increasing population soon outstrips the food supply, causing extreme need; bread is cruelly lacking. The most active, open spirits would turn their mind to some expedient to obviate so serious a condition. If they met together to discuss the matter, we might hear them say that during the time of abundance it did not matter if one individual worked less than another and all received equal portions. No one lacked anything. In the present situation, however, it was not a question of whether people were ready to give benevolently from what was useful to them, but from the necessities of life. If in these

circumstances the land were not divided and the fruits of a person's labour not protected, the whole society would suffer; the food of the weak and hard-working would be stolen and consumed by the strong, lazy and vicious.

28. The argument could be countered by appealing to an increase in land fertility and similar accidents; for example, some portions could eventually far exceed the owner's need. Again this kind of division would initiate exclusive self-love and personal interest: the rich would refuse to give freely from their superfluity and would therefore lord it over the needy. The objection however has no force: the new institution would indeed contain an evil, but an inevitable evil which would be much less than that which left possession open to all. Others would add that although the capacity of the stomach limits the amount of food consumed, people are not likely to give away what they have over when hunger has been satisfied. Instead, they will exchange it for the labour of other members of society, for whom work would be better than death by hunger. In this way, laws of ownership would be established similar to those accepted by all civil peoples. Such laws would be seen not as a means devoid of problems but as the only bulwark against the great evils threatening society.

29. Without considering the *law of ownership* in its moral aspect, dire necessity would inevitably force it on us; either we accept it or devour one another. However, the human race has lived a long time with the benefit of this law, and we must not be surprised at our having eventually lost sight of its importance and meaning for the sake of theories of perfect equality which censure this law as forbidden and harmful — As Godwin and the *Code de la Nature* have done. Guided by our feelings, we note the present minor evils resulting from the law, but ignore the evils from which the law has protected us and to which the law itself has for so long made us insensitive.

30. It will be helpful to pause here for a moment.

I am not ignorant of the objections which can be and are brought against my argument. I appreciate the need to investigate any objections and show that, although attractive, they lack solidity.

31. The first objection denies the continuous growth of population that I have supposed: 'Lack of food is the term posited by

nature to the increase of population. If the population doubles in 25 years, the food supply must also double in the same period. In the second or third 25-year period the population will be static because the food supply cannot increase.'[17] Although the multiplication of the human race does indeed diminish with lack of food, extreme misery would be required to render life impossible and suppress the natural power and law governing the multiplication of the species; normal misery should in fact be sufficient to reduce and check that power. Indeed, where private ownership exists with its inequality of goods, many other causes hold people back from marriage. One such cause is the desire to accumulate wealth and exalt one's family. But when a family has no hope of ever outstripping other families in possessions, and all families hold equal possessions, the income of a large family increases rather than diminishes because the father acquires more right to goods from the community for each of his children. In this case, multiplication is limited only when misery has become universal and extreme. In such a wretched state, the same thing must certainly happen to mankind at large as happens today among the poor classes: multiplication is prevented not so much by the low number of marriages but by hardship, famine, hereditary diseases, so common among the poor, and vice. Unless we blind ourselves, we can easily see what a vile state the earth would be in, home to such wretched and squalid poverty! This would be the inescapable consequence if the law of private ownership, were to be abolished for a long time. It could indeed happen, but only during those brief moments of madness to which God sometimes abandons the nations he wishes to punish; it could never last. Before these extreme

[17] This was indeed Mr. Godwin's objection: 'There is in human society a principle by which the population is continuously maintained at the level of the means of subsistence.' Malthus replies, 'I agree, and I know full well that the millions of excessive population I am speaking about are never static. But the whole question is reduced to knowing what principle holds the balance between population and the means of subsistence. Is it a hidden, vague cause, or a mysterious intervention from heaven that at certain times removes the fruitfulness of marriage? Surely, it is wretchedness, or the fear of wretchedness, the inevitable consequences of natural laws which although tempered, not aggravated by human institutions are not overcome by them.' Romagnosi, in his paper *sulla crescente Popolazione*, did not note this solid reply.

consequences came about, we would sense their full horror as they approached. And if any mad men obstinately supported such a bizarre theory they would become victims of the mob.

32. A second objection has been brought forward by Romagnosi, a respected publicist:[18]

> I do not see how people can generally claim that nature has not provided for the balance between human life and the means of subsistence.[19]

Romagnosi's 'I do not see' clearly has no force to change the laws of nature. We are dealing with a law of fact: nature cannot be called unwise if someone does not see reasons for the law. It is more reasonable to suppose nature endowed with hidden wisdom, deeper than we can plumb.

[18] Romagnosi is fully justified in opposing the opinion of those who would like to abolish charitable homes for illegitimate children under the pretext that such a measure would reduce illegitimate offspring. Even if this were true, it would never suffice to justify such action, cruel and contrary as it is to the Gospel. Romagnosi also opposes those who censure governments that help the poor. But here we must distinguish. Normally charity is a private matter; in my opinion a government may not take money from my pocket to distribute it to the poor. The situation is different, however, in the case of England where the laws themselves make the workers' condition burdensome. The government therefore must compensate with the poor tax which, considered as a form of governmental restitution, becomes a necessary remedy and a kind of satisfaction. Romagnosi after referring to the oppressive English laws affecting workers and dating from as long ago as Henry VII, says with great acumen: 'Surely this condition of the English workers constitutes a real servitude in factories, exactly the same as that of the glebe? They were supported by a poor tax, just as the slave of the glebe, tied with the ox and horse to the soil, had to be maintained' (*Del trattamento dei poveri della libertà commerciale*, etc., Milan, 1829). Thirdly, Romagnosi opposed the enforced prohibition of marriage among the poor. I too have shown the injustice and unreasonableness of this in *Discorso sul Celibato*, reprinted many times.

Although I agree fully or partially with Romagnosi in all this, I must point out that these questions differ from the fundamental problem of the increase of population and the need for a radical solution. Romagnosi, confusing this question with the other three, arms himself with all that is repulsive in the first three when settled in a Malthusian way. The last question, for which alone we praise the merits of *Saggio sulla Popolazione*, suffers as a consequence.

[19] *Sulla crescente Popolazione, Memoria di G. D. Romagnosi*, Milan, 1830.

Let us grant that the imbalance between the means of subsistence and the reproductive force of the species gives the impression that the imbalance comes directly from nature, not from a disorder produced in nature by the human will. In this case, it is religion which explains this and many other mysteries found in the present state of things.

Thirdly, provident nature has been able to compensate for the disorder caused by guilty human beings. In the beginning, nature did not insert in us only a reproductive force (in which case reproduction would have been mechanical, or rather animal); it united reason and freedom to our reproductive force. These are the sublime faculties which have to rule all the other inferior faculties, with the consequent direction, moderation and limitation of our reproductive force.[20] Furthermore, the Creator of nature, by means of our spiritual regeneration through a new force called 'grace', rehabilitated our injured reason, as it were, so that it could exercise its sovereign rights, and made possible dominion over our lower faculties in our fallen state. This exercise, which had always been a natural duty, was not matched in our unregenerated state by the power to carry it out although this the only satisfactory solution to the great problem of the celibacy of the poor lies here.[21]

33. This provides the answer to Romagnosi's second objection which follows from his first. He says:

> The kingdom of God on earth consists in the universal observance of justice. Can this justice be exercised with

[20] Hence the following words of Romagnosi have no sense: 'These gentlemen suppose...that the Supreme Ordainer and Ruler of nature has disposed things in such a way that creatures are born without provision for the means to preserve them during the possible course of their life.' These words would have some meaning if God had ordained that every human being should reproduce. And this does seem what Romagnosi intends. He goes on: 'I say that a new-born baby can be suffocated according to the same right by which, with necessity as our excuse, we forbid a fellow human being *to obey the natural and divine precept to reproduce another human being*.' But these words must surely have a meaning other than their literal meaning, spoken as they are by a celibate!

[21] Cf. above, my *Discorso sul Celibato*, where I show how the spirit of the Church gently and caringly regulates and orders the question of celibacy to the advantage of human society.

> greed, pride and inhumanity rather than with affability, fellowship and the practice of sincere civil sociality? It is precisely in the latter conditions that the kingdom of God and his justice is found. Under such conditions the increase of population can never become fearful or require excessive moral constraint.[22]

34. Romagnosi is appealing to Jesus Christ. We must therefore interpret carefully what Jesus Christ says ('Seek first the kingdom of God and his justice, and all these things shall be added unto you') in accordance with the spirit of the God-Man and the whole of his teaching. Affability, fellowship, and true civil society are indeed conditions of the kingdom of God on the earth, but they are certainly not the only conditions demanded by the kingdom of God preached by Jesus Christ. They alone could not be a remedy for the natural law of reproduction, nor for the imbalance between population which increases in geometric progression, and the means of subsistence which increase in arithmetical progression, unless we wanted to posit a miracle, or supposed that human beings would abstain from excessive reproduction through affability, fellowship and love of sociality. Romagnosi however is not disposed to grant this kind of moderation. On the contrary, he says that the kingdom of God cannot require excessive moral constraint. We must note therefore that this teaching of Romagnosi (that the kingdom of God does not require the most difficult act of moral constraint) scarcely accords with Christ's saying that 'men of violence take the kingdom of God by force';[23] it has little in common with teaching of the greatest generosity which declares continence (something unheard of on earth!) to be sublime virtue and numbered among the counsels to be followed by those who wish to be perfect.

35. We fully agree that those who seek first the kingdom of God and his justice will certainly never lack what is necessary even in this life. But this is due not to any absence of highly difficult moral constraint, as Romagnosi evidently believes. The opposite is true: the just will apply the constraint to themselves, and will obtain the power to do so. This constraint will become

22 *Sulla crescente Popolazione.*

23 Mt 11: [12].

incredibly easy for them and be compensated by interior delights of the spirit much more satisfying than those of the flesh. In short, the just will not practise Malthus' *moral restraint* nor the *legal restraint* imposed arbitrarily by the strong on the weak,[24] but *Christian celibacy*, that is, a spontaneous continence, holy and blessed for all who practise it, more valuable than any treasure and far more delightful than every pleasure; a continence which transforms people into angels not by an extraordinary miracle — it occurs every day, everywhere and all the time in the Church of Jesus Christ — but nevertheless by a stupendous miracle, unbelievable to those who do not know the power of the grace of the Redeemer. They do not believe in this grace, although it is visible to them every day; they deride it because they neither can, nor wish to believe in it! [*App*., no. 1]

36. II. Let us now consider the law governing marriages, which, as we have said, is the second constitutive law of society.

History shows that the law of marriage is as old as human society, and that whenever a population wanted to rise to a state of community from the barbaric, errant state to which it had fallen, a necessary first step was to subject the union of the sexes to stable regulations, and in this way to institute true, inviolable marriages.

But while this is true, only a sound philosophy can reveal its intimate reason and absolute necessity. Today, there are some who fail to see this reason and necessity because, at such a distance from social beginnings, they no longer appreciate the supreme need which, as I have said, confronted the founders of communities, the legislators or, so to speak, the helmsmen.

37. If the law which stabilised and sanctified marital unions were not rooted in moral dictates, social necessity alone, it

[24] Among the strangest constraints imaginable for preventing the propagation of the species, nothing is more ridiculous than that proposed recently by Weinhold, doctor of philosophy, medicine and surgery, and professor at the university of Halle in Prussia. In a work entitled *Dell'eccessa di popolazione nell'Europa*, Halle, 1827, he suggests a physical instrument, a kind of castration to be carried out on all the poor by public decree and reinforced by an official seal to prevent every act of procreation. I do not know if it was a serious proposal or just a joke! But we are bound to descend to such folly, or more accurately, such depravity, once we desert the only social and human system, that is, the Catholic system.

seems to me, would have given rise to it. This necessity is of many kinds: the necessity founded in the indivisible nature of love; the necessity according to which human beings wish to ensure that they see themselves and their own reflection mirrored in their children; the necessity that urges human beings to safeguard the life they themselves have given to their children. Some nations might break the sacred bonds which make marriage human and secure so that the will of imprudent people, desirous of some accidental advantage uppermost in their thoughts, might prevail. Such people could indeed be blind to everything that a law regulating marriage ought to contain, necessarily and indispensably, for the existence of a human, civil association. Very soon, the disorder afflicting family society (the foundation of civil society) and the confusion resulting from this disorder would make the members aware that the new measures had affected and removed one of the firmest foundations of human communal living. The evils they experienced would teach them once more to recognise the wisdom of those who first enacted and sanctioned the marital laws.

In the imaginary assembly we spoke about earlier, fathers of families would propose the absolute need to return to the ancient institution; the more prudent would add 'that the certainty of seeing children supported by social benevolence detracts from the effort to make the land produce enough for the increasing population. Even if this certainty did not induce laziness, and all applied themselves intently to their work, the population could still increase infinitely more quickly than the increase in produce. It would be necessary therefore to apply some restraint to human reproduction, and the simplest, most natural would be, it seems, to oblige each father to acknowledge and feed his own children.

Such a law would inevitably act as a regulator and curtailer of the population, because no one would wish to bring unfortunate creatures into the world whom he would be unable to feed. But if anyone did so, it would be just for him to bear the evils of his inconsidered action, and the complaints of his starving children (if they were capable of complaining) would have to be borne solely by the improvident author of their wretched existence. Hence, generally speaking, anyone who loved work, would obtain the right to multiply his own kind, a right which would never be disturbed; the indolent and imprudent, in usurping such a right, would be punished by their own sloth.'

38. From all this we can rightly conclude that the great error of the inventors of the empty theories we have discussed is 'to attribute to human institutions all the vices and calamities which upset society. — The facts however demonstrate that the evils caused by human institutions (and some of the evils are indeed real) must be seen as minor and superficial in comparison with those arising from the laws of limited nature and from human passions.'[25]

[25] Malthus, *Essai sur la Population*, bk. 3, c. 1.

CHAPTER 5

How respect for antiquity and love of useful innovations must be regulated

39. The supreme respect we see given throughout history and by all nations to their first institutions has therefore a deep reason.[26] Some so-called philosophers ridiculed this respect, declaring it blind ignorance and servile obsequiousness to authority; in short, stupidity. They did not see the reason for this respect. They did not understand that it is an effect of a principle of nature, an effect of a rational law; that there is something deeper in the common sense of nations than in the empty theories of a few individuals, and that our vision, guided by a series of experiences from the distant past, is more likely to see what is true than an imagination unbridled by facts, which roams about in the world of the unusual and of the possible.

Let us therefore be convinced that the first institutions are necessarily those on which a society is founded. The founders had to attend to bringing into existence what did not exist; they had no time to think about accessories.

40. We should not be deceived. This natural, wise respect does not oblige us to oppose useful innovations, but to distinguish accurately between innovations which *destroy* what is old, and innovations which *add* to what is old. Relative to those which are aimed at destroying anything ancient, we must proceed with greater diffidence and caution. The innovators must be certain that they are destroying merely a prop or scaffolding, not a principal arch or a column. Relative to innovations which add but do not destroy, and therefore entail less danger of harming

[26] The cause I have given for the honour paid by human beings to antiquity does not exclude other causes. Religion, the natural piety of children towards their fathers, the need we generally feel to cling to an authority rather than flounder in uncertainty, the instinct for universal sociality by which we desire to live united with those who have passed on and those yet to come, and similar causes also play a part.

a society's existence, we must act in such a way that what is new harmonises well with the old and corresponds to the toothing left by the first builders.

CHAPTER 6

The meaning of the rule: 'a society must often return to its beginning' if it is to survive.

41. Similarly, our teaching shows how a positive, and even deep meaning can be given to Machiavelli's well-known observation: 'If a sect or republic is to survive for any length of time, it must return frequently to its beginning.'[27] This rule requires the prolongation of the first and second periods in the existence of States, that is, their periods of *foundation* and *legislation*, so that States may be renewed before they begin to degenerate. About republics, he says:

> This return to the beginning is brought about by an external accident or by internal prudence. Relative to the former, we see how necessary it was for Rome to be taken by the French so that it could be reborn, regain new life and power, and once again exercise religion and justice, which had begun to degenerate.

And concerning internal accidents:

> These must originate either from a law which frequently reviews matters for the members of the society, or from someone born in the society who by his example and virtuous actions produces the same effect as the law.

This political maxim was already followed in Italy at the time of the republics when noble concepts and sublime virtues, mixed with atrocious vices, shone forth, and later in the Florentine republic.

> Those who governed the state of Florence from 1434 till 1494 relate, in connection with this, how every five years it was necessary to renew the State, which otherwise was difficult to preserve. What they called renewal meant implanting in the people the terror and fear implanted at the

[27] *Discorsi sopra la prima Deca di T. Livio*, bk. 3, c. 1.

founding of the State, when those were struck down who, judged by the way of living at the time, had acted wrongly.[28]

42. Nor could things be different in the Church, the greatest society of all, which God generally preserves through secondary causes without the constant intervention of miracles. Thus, this most wise society, whose foundation was laid by wisdom itself, always had as its supreme, most faithful guide the rule about returning to antiquity, a rule expressed in these words of Tertullian: 'Christian society is grounded entirely in holy antiquity, and its ruinous state cannot be more securely rectified than by consideration of its origin.'[29] Machiavelli notes: 'If it had not been taken back to its beginning by St. Francis or St. Dominic' (or, in my opinion, by some other divine means) 'it would have been totally annihilated.'

[28] *Ibid.*

[29] *Contra Marcionem*, bk. 1, c. 13.

CHAPTER 7

Our criterion applied to the four stages

43. Let us now return to our subject and summarise what we have said. The first institutions are concerned with *substance*, the second, *accidents*; the primary need is to exist; the second, to enjoy the fruits of existence.

44. When the time has come for the institutions concerned with the accidental good of a society, the need to exist, which has so to speak been satisfied, is no longer felt. The essential, fundamental institutions are still in force through habit, not through an actual, urgent need as in the beginning. Habit however removes not only the force of sensations but distracts attention from reflection on the reasons for things. Wherever habit replaces deliberate attention to reality, the reason for the creation of the institutions is soon forgotten. Ancient institutions are no longer understood or intelligently maintained; only inveterate custom preserves them.

45. Many evils result from this and in a hidden way alter the State. Finally a time comes when we tire of acting mechanically; our oppressed understanding begins to long to return to its natural duty and becomes once more the guide of those enslaved for so long to ancient, obscure customs.[30] To this noble voice of

[30] Today we are a long way from the time of the *founders* and *institutors* of civil societies. However we have seen in our days a man who could be called the founder of a new society in Europe. He had to deal with the same principles as the heads of primitive societies. Properly speaking, this cannot be credited to his intelligence, as some believe. It is an effect of the nature of the situation. Napoleon's comments were the same as ours. The following excerpts, taken from *Manoscritto di Sant'Elena*, certainly express thoughts similar to his, and demonstrate his agreement with our own theory. — Page 40: 'March 31st. proved how difficult it was, rather than easy, to make the old and new regimes live together in peace.' — P. 44: 'They had no doubt that my rule bore no relationship at all to theirs. Mine rested totally on facts; theirs, solely on rights. Theirs was founded ONLY ON CUSTOM; MINE DID AWAY WITH CUSTOM and marched in line with the spirit of the age which they wanted to hold in check.' — P. 68: 'I could not

reason desiring once more to exercise its rights, we can add the power of self-love spurring our minds to the discovery of new things. Prejudices, passions and a desire for sophistication can also reveal themselves in many people, who then have a wider field in which to give free rein to their immoderate desires. In these circumstances, ancient institutions, the target of so many conspiring forces and assaults, easily begin to succumb. Only an empty shell remains; the core, or reason for the original establishment of the institutions is no longer remembered.

46. At this stage, when the oldest institutions are assailed, the majority of people readily and naturally follow the standard raised by the new party. They consider the old institutions no longer defensible; as far as they can see, the attack is simply against the outmoded prejudices and useless relics of an ignorant, primitive age. But beside the majority there are some who are obstinately blind, others who through laziness retain the old practices, and others again who rightly sense they must be faithful to the past but are unable to explain why. Finally, there are a few who with great wisdom not only see why the majority are deceived but indicate the falsehood of the new teachings; they are able to reveal the ancient origins of the practices and show how their ancestors established them not so much as a result of wisdom but by force of necessity.

However this tiny minority (the vast majority often go to the opposite extreme) may fail to convince the multitude not to rebel openly against the old institutions. In addition, even those (fortunately a large number) who publicly proclaim and dem-

carry out anything on the basis of custom and illusion. I was obliged to create everything out of some kind of reality. Thus it was necessary to found my legislation on the immediate interests of the majority, and create my organisations on the basis of interest, because interests are what is most real in this world.' — P. 69: 'The old nobility depended for its existence on its prerogatives; mine had nothing but power. The merit of the old was simply its exclusivity. All those who distinguished themselves entered by right into the new nobility, which was solely a reward for civic service; the people attached no other meaning to it. Each one had merited it by his actions, and all could obtain it at the same price; it was contemptuous of no one.' — P. 77: 'The empire had acquired an immense superiority through the Battle of Jena. The public began to regard my cause as vindicated, and I noticed this by the comportment of others towards me. I began to believe it myself, and this favourable impression caused me to make mistakes.'

onstrate in favour of preserving for a little longer the old institutions which they practise by force of habit may fail to convince the others. The same may befall those who through an intimate feeling for what is right are either immune to the new sophisms, which they do not understand, or unaffected by the novelty which seeks to shake them out of their laziness.

As a result of all this, society itself is shaken and made unstable. People now begin to feel the need for those ancient foundations of which they are so ignorant. Unable to accept meekly the total destruction of their society, they find themselves in the same state as their predecessors. In this state, it is not great wisdom (they have rejected wisdom and closed their ears to the warnings of prudent minds) but a harsh, ineluctable need that turns them to reconstruct what they have destroyed, to restore the things of the past, and to acknowledge or rather experience their usefulness. At such a time the institutions take on a new consistency and solidity; they are maintained and respected rationally, not habitually, and so give birth once more to human society.

47. What we have said describes the events of recent times. We can understand now that certain wise people have not condemned the modern age and mourned the past without foundation. Because of the early need to establish society, stronger and more solid institutions had obviously to be created from the start. But this does not allow us to consider lightly subsequent rulers of civil associations. Even when those who came later were of equal or greater intelligence, the nature of the case would have made them less remarkable; they were playing a minor theme, which gave them scope for virtuosity; what was substantial had already been attended to. Inevitably their only concern was to complete the work and adorn it with more detailed, ordered forms. The trunk of a tree divides into branches and fronds, but its form and completion is given by the foliage that clothes it. The foliage may indeed be less valuable than the trunk, but to require the tree to grow new trunks in place of the foliage would be unreasonable. The leaves must not be considered separately from the whole tree. Without the tree they would look very strange; joined to the tree they make the plant brighter and more majestic. The error of those who ceaselessly complain and moan about the rulers of civil and ecclesiastical

societies, and affect an immoderate, blind love for antiquity (we presume that their devotion to the past is totally sincere and free of secondary aims), shows the kind of narrow vision which views the foliage separately from the trunk, and is upset to see that the great, perfectly formed tree, instead of putting out new branches, forms new leaves, blossom and fruit at its extremities.

48. But enough of that; we must now briefly summarise what we have said about the laws governing the progress of all human societies, as we have described them so far.

In every society, four principal stages or periods can be distinguished. Similarly, the political criterion we have posited is seen gradually to undergo four vicissitudes.

1st social stage. This stage concerns the existence of a society, when only its *substance* is considered. It is divided into two periods: *foundation* and *legislation*.

2nd social stage. This is the stage of development after existence has been assured. Although attention is now given to *accidents*, *substance* is not lost sight of. In this period nations, after becoming great, are embellished in every way and seen, by both the foreigner and its own members, in all its brilliant splendour.

3rd social stage. At this stage, the citizens are dazzled by the external pomp and by all that has rendered nations attractive and delightful rather than strong. They begin to lose sight of all that is *substantial*; a spirit of levity and over-confidence reveals itself. This period is one of degeneration and corruption for society.

4th social stage. The preoccupation of society's members with frivolous objects eats away at the foundations on which the first builders constructed the edifice; the fourth accident to which the State is subject replaces the third. In this fourth period society is shaken either by attacks from external enemies or by internal upheavals, and its very existence is threatened.

49. In this very important period the State undoubtedly suffers a crisis or great change, which no human force can prevent. Once a society has reached this point it can no longer go back: it can only hope that the crisis be prolonged; it will never be overcome. In this period, the State is either completely destroyed, losing its freedom and becoming subject to an external enemy, or (granted great power and good fortune enabling it to

resist external assaults and internal disorder.) renews and purges itself after terrible upheavals, receiving almost another existence. In this case it has taken a step forward in civilization and political prosperity, a step made at the price of mortal suffering, bloody sacrifices and countless victims but written with a clear sign of grace in the eternal book of Providence.

CHAPTER 8

Societies are judged according to *practical* and *speculative* reason. — Application of the political criterion to the *practical reason* of the masses

50. It would be interesting and useful to ask here: 'What are the laws according to which the political criterion we have mentioned gradually loses its importance in the eyes of people until completely forgotten?' In other words, 'What are the laws according to which societies move from careful attention to their existence, a characteristic of their first stage, to the three other successive stages which we have indicated?'

51. This investigation can be conducted from two points of view because civil societies are moved by two forces which, although never entirely separate, never work with equal efficacy. Sometimes one, sometimes the other is prevalent. In this way, they characterise and constitute two different states in civil society.

These two forces are the *practical reason of the masses*, and the *speculative reason of the individuals* who direct society.

52. The practical reason of a society, by which the masses are guided, could also be called, although improperly, *social instinct*. It resembles instinct in the sense that difficulties arise when we try to indicate the precise reasons leading the masses to operate socially. These reasons are undoubtedly present and serve as a secret guide to what the masses do, although even the masses themselves are unable to express or formulate them. However, they are not the object of reflection on the part of the masses. Such reflection would be necessary if the people as whole are to be capable of explaining and expressing them. We also have to consider that these reasons are neither general nor result from great foresight. *Remoter* effects and even *universal* effects never enter the heads of the general run of people who are motivated to act by present, immediate advantage, which constitutes the practical reason we are discussing.

53. At this point, a question arises: 'If the masses do not act according to some prevision of *distant* effects, nor calculate the *general* effects, how is it that they sometimes give signs of possessing an infallible instinct? Why is their action often far more sensible than that of high-ranking politicians, and their tendency such that it has often formed the greatness of nations and kingdoms?'

This an important question, and forms part of our investigation: 'What are the laws by which societies pass from directing themselves according to the rule about substance and accident, which we have mentioned, to the point at which they totally lose sight of this faithful guide?'

54. We note, in fact, that the infallible instinct of the masses is not always evident. It shows itself only at certain times and in certain states of society, and depends on the following contingency: 'The people act socially to strengthen and maintain their society if, in their eyes, the immediate good which constitutes the stimulus and motive of their activity is one with the good itself of the society, and especially with the good which makes it subsist. At this point, the action of the masses appears to possess great foresight and wisdom because it brings in its wake highly beneficial, long-term and universal effects. These, however, are not the effects of foresight and calculation on the part of the people because the very nature itself of the situation has led and forced them to act in that way. In this case the present, particular good, at which the people are aiming, is *per accidens* the selfsame good forming the support of the society and containing the seed of its development. In such an event, it is usual to attribute to the wisdom of the people what is simply the wisdom of nature. We normally speak about an instinct of foresight only in the case of excellent, long-term, universal effects. These, however, are obtained not in fact by human foresight, but by a natural connection between what human beings do and the consequences of their action. There is no need for people to have seen the connection, natural forces act even if unseen.'

55. We shall understand the circumstances and laws according to which the activity of the masses first conforms to the criterion we have explained, and then gradually departs from it, if we ask: 'What are the immediate benefits presented as desirable to the

eyes of the masses at different times and in different states of society?'

56. Here it would be easy to note how, in the beginning, the very existence of the society is the good seen immediately and vividly by all, just as the destruction of the society is the immediate evil present to the masses. In fact, the infancy of a society is always an eminently *patriotic* epoch, as it were. The good of each person, considered as a member of the social unit, is equivalent to the elementary good itself of society.[31]

57. Secondly, we can note how this good of existence becomes *remote* rather than immediate when the foundation of a society is complete and its existence secure. At such a moment the immediate, obtainable benefits are those which pertain to the development of the society itself, and its power and glory. *Love of one's country* changes because the country's glory and dignity are more obvious than its existence.

58. After a society has developed and gained prestige, while enjoying these benefits at length, and exhausting the forces it has devoted to their acquisition, the desire of its members — always eager for novelty — turns naturally to love of tranquil, peaceful pleasures. This is the period of luxury and enjoyment, which now become the *immediate* good to which the masses tend and according to which they operate.

This period of decadence does at first preserve a kind of *patriotism* which desires peace, wealth and pleasure for the country. Such patriotism is as yielding as its object, and as weak as the will from which it sprang. Soon, patriotism is accompanied by inertia, which increases along with luxury and the abuse of pleasures. Finally, this voluptuous inertia takes forms indicative of *selfishness* which first threatens and then suffocates *patriotism*. All generous feeling subsides in the spirit, given over now to contempt for those who have gone before. The nation, which has entirely lost sight of the rule that we have posited, is blind to every good proper to the country and devotes its attention to individual good alone, around which it girates briefly before its final collapse. Poets, who always express the

[31] This explains why patriotism is more strongly asserted and augmented in times of war when the existence of nations is endangered.

state of a society, sing as Ovid once did, not without presumption but certainly without shame:

Let others turn back for help to our origins;
I am so glad to be born now. This age suits me
Not because pliant gold is drawn from the earth,
And the sea-shell vessels we behold have come from other lands;
Nor because mountains shrink as we excavate our marble,
And our jetties hold back the blue waters —
No! We have our own style of living
And the pitiful rustic life of our ancestors has gone.[32]

This state comes to an end along with that in which the ultimate, single thought of the people is directed to 'bread and circuses'. Everyone can see that history supports all that I have said.

[32] *De A.*, 3: 121-128.

CHAPTER 9

Continuation: an explanation of conquests

59. We have to note in passing that not all peoples undergo at the same time the various stages we have distinguished. Some move more quickly than others; some stay at one stage longer than others. As a result, it is possible to find contemporaneous peoples, one of which is at the first stage, while another has already arrived at the third or fourth stage. And this explains conquests.

It is in fact evident that any nation in the first or second of the stages we have posited possesses a great advantage over another people already at the third or fourth stage. Let us take for example the fall of the western Roman Empire at the hands of the Germanic peoples, as described by a recent author in words which serve my purpose exactly. He notes with some precision that the Germanic nations did not conquer the Roman world with overpowering force, as is commonly supposed. They possessed neither a huge population, nor political institutions, nor military discipline; they conquered because they

> existed in the first centuries of our era, that is, at the height and decadence of other civilisations around the Mediterranean. At that time, the Germanic peoples experienced the same social state that the others had undergone eight or ten centuries previously. In other words, they were at the stage of *city-states*, that is of tiny, separate peoples who came together for short periods in constantly changing federations.[33]

This is exactly the point I am making when I say that civil society, although still not fully constituted, cannot lose sight of its being. On the contrary, this is the one thing present to the masses at this period of time, and their only driving force.

[33] *Della Letturatura negli XI primi secoli dell'Era Cristiana, Lettere di C. Balbo*, Turin, 1836, Lett. 2.

Balbo also notes wisely that even relative to force and natural vigour the advantage remained with the Mediterranean nations:

> The Pelasgic, Celtic and Germanic peoples were always defeated by the Mediterranean nations who, despite enjoying the same civic state as their foes, pushed these back and kept them locked up in their wildernesses. They were only conquered when the other peoples had progressed to a further state of civilisation which, however, presented deficiencies and difficulties. At this point, the more developed peoples experienced all the disadvantages of their new position without having acquired any of the advantages incompatible with a period in which the process of civilisation was so striking.[34]

60. The deficiency and incapacities of this new state of civilisation will be found to consist, in my well-considered opinion, in the fact that peoples had arrived at conditions in which the immediate good for which they were working was no longer existence or the glory of their country or even something accessory to the social good, but the good of the individual. The Germans on the other hand, although at a much lower stage of development, were in a condition where the nature of the matter in hand offered them the existence and glory of their association as the object to be attained. This is precisely the state described by our author when he speaks of the Germans and other peoples. Let us listen once more to his accurate, astute comments. Speaking of the Germans, he says:

> Other than minor moral corruption, the condition in which the *city-states* remained gave them immense advantages over populations which had long since made further progress. In the *city-state* every citizen was always a soldier (*Heerman* or *Wehrmann*). Amongst his own people he was free, as we said, but outside his people he was a tyrant, and thus forced to carry arms in war and peace. In this social state, war is the natural condition of human beings, and there is no doubt that such was the case in the ancient world — another difference between the ancient and modern worlds. For this reason warlike qualities such as courage, *virtus*, and love of one's city were the principal, if not the only virtues in antiquity. So, too, constant deteriora-

[34] *Ibid.*

> tion was the fate of ancient societies which gradually distanced themselves from the city-state and from a state of constant warfare. The supreme aim and success of the ancient legislators, such as Lycurgus and Romulus, was to preserve the nation as a city-state, and to pursue constant warfare. On all sides, 'outsider' and 'foreigner' were synonymous. The Jewish enmity for everyone other than their own people was a factor common to all nations; everyone divided the world into two parts only: his own people or city, and the other peoples, peoples in general.

61. He goes on:

> Germany, which had remained at this stage, conquered not only the Romans, who had unfortunately progressed from that stage, but also the Huns and other Asian nations which had either not come so far or had themselves burst forth at the time of the immense empire of Attila and his predecessors.[35]

62. We can conclude, therefore, that the law according to which our criterion of substance and accident is in fact observed relative to the masses or multitudes 'consists in a constant deterioration (which points to the truth of the saying: "the older the world, the worse it gets") or in a succession of different states of a nation as it passes in its early years from complete, faithful observance of the rule to gradual, constant neglect and eventual total forgetfulness of it.'

[35] *Ibid.*

CHAPTER 10

Application of the political criterion to the *speculative reason* of influential individuals

63. So far we have considered the history of our criterion in the light of its relationship with the *practical reason* of the masses. We now have to consider it in its relationship with the *speculative reason* of individuals who exercise most influence in the government of societies. In other words, we have to consider it in relationship to the educated human spirit, and thus trace the progress by which humanity makes itself ever more capable of using such a criterion.

64. Consideration of the history of our criterion relative to the use made of it by the *masses* is of great importance with respect to non-Christian civil societies; the same consideration relative to well educated, influential *individuals* or to individuals who govern, is more appropriate to Christian societies.

65. Careful observation will show that one of the characteristics of non-Christian societies is to be guided for the most part by the practical reason of the masses. This occurs because those who enjoy power in such societies know how to exercise it only in harmony with the practical reason of the masses. Generally speaking, these rulers are incapable of acting in opposition to such reason. As a result, the destruction of these societies, once they have taken a turn for the worse, is inevitable. There is no human power to hold them back on their fatal journey.

In Christian societies, on the other hand, we find the kind of mentality and culture which raises individuals above the masses. Separated from the masses, they possess a totally new energy with which, in favourable circumstances, they are capable of effectively opposing the blind movement of the masses. The spirit of Christianity is something more than human and as such does not disregard or connive at any error or weakness, or blind, harmful inclination. Such a sublime and truly supernatural spirit has the *courage* and power to hold out against public opinion and gain the favour of the masses by enlightening, restraining and guiding them. This is unheard of in the history of non-Christian societies. The courage we are speaking of is superhuman, the power mysterious. It saves societies when they are heading to dissolution; it gives them lasting life, renewing them in the midst of the greatest adversities and misadventures; it is that which underlies the words: 'God made the nations of the earth healable.'

66. Clearly, relative to Christian culture, the use of the rule we have indicated must proceed in a way contrary to its progression amongst the masses. Relative to Christianity, its progression must be *ascendant* in the sense that the human spirit constantly advances in knowledge of the importance of the rule, and constantly renders itself more capable of practising it.

We have now to investigate the nature of this law according to which progress is continually being made. It is as follows.

67. We must distinguish two kinds of perfection in our faculty of knowledge. One is perfection dependent upon a large number of well-ordered notions, which makes the faculty capable of great 'breadth of calculation'. The other is perfection dependent upon the faculty's power of abstraction, which makes it capable of great 'height of abstraction'. Human capacity for making use of the rule of which we are speaking is in proportion to the development of these two perfections of the faculty of knowledge.

68. *Breadth of calculation* leads human beings to realise with greater certainty which of the two parts of society is *substantial* (the part on which we *have* to concentrate) and which *accessory*.

69. 'Height of abstraction' then becomes necessary if we are to make a perfect division between the substantial and accidental parts. Without this, non-substantial matters could easily be retained along with what is substantial, and insisted upon with excessive rigour. This is the source of oppressive laws and arbitrary limitations imposed on human development; in short, it produces very serious impediments, with which short-sighted authority blocks the natural progress of accidental, but praiseworthy and valuable social benefits.

70. Normally the acquisition of *breadth of calculation* is proper to those whose ambit of affairs is more extended, that is, to

people who are members of wider societies. Others, accustomed to government on a small scale, are usually restricted to very limited political calculation — unless their own ingenuity takes them further than their real circumstances. They are used to thinking only of themselves and their own restricted ambient. They judge the world from their own point of view, and naturally fall into many errors. They are easily inclined to petty competition, base acts of pride and unceasing rivalry. It is easy to see that perpetual subdivision of government in a nation leads to a desire for independence and supremacy on the part of cities, none of which knows how to prefer the good of the whole to that of a part. When little States are destroyed, they want to rise again and possibly celebrate their animosity towards others with vendettas. They pay no attention to common development which would flower to the extent that States of any great region were reduced in number and enlarged.[36]

71. The *faculty of abstraction* grows in people, taken as a whole, as a result of the work of centuries.

It is certain that at first people do not know how to make use of *abstraction*. Their intelligence, constricted by their imagination, is focused on *beings* themselves, not on the *reasons* explaining beings, that is, on their qualities and relationships. For example, people do not at first reflect greatly on the reason or abstract concept of a human being, but on subsistent human beings — Tom, Dick and Harry. As a result, their calculations generally have the advantage of paying attention to *substance*

[36] Signor Pareto wrote to Lord Castlereagh on May 11th 1814 on behalf of Genoa: 'The true force of States consists in union and harmony amongst their citizens. Consequently the association into a single State of PEOPLE SO CONSISTENTLY CONTRARY AND ADVERSE TO ONE ANOTHER AS LIGURIANS AND PIEDMONTESE would undoubtedly weaken rather than strengthen them.' Serra, in a Note to the Congress of Vienna, said: 'If the life of the people is not to be contrary to the decisions [of the Congress of Vienna], at least the independence of Genoa will have to be safeguarded by its being granted a Sovereign who, like the Kings of Tuscany and Modena and those who first ruled Parma and Piacenza, is related to the great governing families of Europe. The evils flowing from foreign rule have been so recently and profoundly inflicted upon the Genovese that this people could never submit again without repugnance and complaint.' The final words show that the Italians of Genoa considered domination by the Italians in Turin to be on a par with domination by the French.'

because they are incapable of separating what is *accidental* from the substance. But this also brings them to sacrifice many accessory matters and to establish excessively rigid and partly arbitrary dispositions.

72. After this first period, but as a result of Christianity to which the next development is normally owed, there follows a greater ease of abstraction, and separation of accidents from substance. This step leads people to perfect their way of ruling themselves; they know how to separate accidents from substance and consequently tend to attain substance without sacrificing accidents or blocking their development. It is true that such distinctions, when abused, open the way to subtlety and sophistication which, in its turn, gives rise to error and finally to excessive attachment to what is accidental in public affairs. This deficiency is not irreparable, however, granted the presence of *breadth* and *power of calculation* sufficient to remedy it.

73. In general we can say that ancient errors sprang from lack of distinctions; modern errors from an over-abundance of distinctions. The desire to be perfect and safeguard accidents easily leads us to abandon substance.

This provides one explanation for the ancient tendency to excessive servitude and the modern inclination to excessive freedom. The former error sprang from too little abstraction or distinction in considering human relationships; the latter from too much. This teaching is more important than we generally realise. It is the key enabling us to understand and explain the facts and customs of the earliest times of the human race.

74. We conclude, therefore: we have indicated two ways in which, as *societies grow* and *time passes*, mankind places itself in an ever better position to use our political rule or criterion: 1. by the acquisition of a greater breadth of calculation, and 2. by a higher degree of abstraction.

CHAPTER 11

Relationships in public affairs between the action of *speculative reason* in individuals, and the contemporaneous action of *practical reason* in the masses

75. Until now, we have considered our political criterion in the circumstances to which it is subject as a result of the twofold progress of the human spirit. We have seen that human understanding, as it acquires *breadth of calculation*, learns how to put the whole before the parts but, as it acquires *height of abstraction* and consequently runs a risk of neglecting substance through fallacious love of accidents, becomes simultaneously more capable of prudent use of the criterion of substance. This enables it to safeguard substance itself and leave accidents to their own natural progress.

76. Here we have to consider that modern nations, despite the seeds of Christian culture sown in them, suffer the vicissitudes of politics. This culture, of which we have already spoken, does indeed save them at times from the edge of the abyss, but it does not obviate political difficulties. There is a contrast between *ascending progression,* in the case of the speculative reason of those who govern, and *descending progression,* in the case of the practical reason of the masses, that is, relative to the earthy, grosser part of society. The ascending progression constantly prevails over the descending, however.

77. These two forces of speculative reason on the part of the more educated, and of practical reason on the grosser part (in other words, the reason of individuals and of the masses) operate simultaneously and as it were in parallel. The contemporaneous and sometimes contrasting action of the two forces explains why Christian societies are often storm-tossed without suffering total shipwreck, especially if Christianity is considered as a single society in which individual nations are simply members.

78. With this in mind, it will not be out of place to note the reasons according to which the use of our criterion of substance and accidents is gradually abandoned, only to be taken up again in the differing states to which Christian nations are subject.

79. I note first that substantial institutions are lost sight of

1. in proportion to their antiquity;
2. in proportion to the increase in the multiplicity of accidental institutions.

80. Clearly, the *length of time* during which substantial institutions have existed will contribute to forgetfulness of the impelling necessity which brought them into being. In this regard, the nation, if capable of renewal (and granted that it is destined to be punished, not annihilated), simply undergoes a crisis whose purpose is to draw ideas together once more. In this case, there is no need to recall accidental institutions and any external activity because they are continually present. In the order of providence, the crisis is intended as a reminder of the reason for the ancient institutions, and undoubtedly achieves its aim. As soon as the memory is re-activated, ancient institutions are reunited with modern practices. As a result, the system is completed in human understanding; knowledge is advanced and society ameliorated.

81. In Christian nations, which possess an interior philosophy of renewal and are not destined to perish, this process normally takes place within three generations (the minimum period required).

82. In the first generation, when the reasons for the ancient institutions are already forgotten, people rebel against the institutions and overthrow them more or less quickly.

83. The second generation now finds the society in a state of agitation and decomposition, and, through lack of its old supports, in danger of total ruin. But this generation is anxious and diffident about novelty and, after coming to its senses, raises once more the fallen institutions. It re-founds the society on its shaken foundations; it devotes itself totally to this aim while taking little notice of its accessory parts. Machiavelli indicates what is at stake when he says:

> True virtue is sought in difficult times; when times are easy,

> it is not the virtuous but the rich and well-placed who find favour.[37]

This shows that in the second, fortunate period of which we are speaking, attention is given not to what is *essential* but to the accidentals which surround people, such as external splendour. When times are difficult, people return once more to what is solid and effective.

84. Finally, the third generation appears, enriched with the experience of the two preceding generations. Now that passions have been tempered on the one hand, and the yoke of habit broken on the other, this generation has a noble, joyful mission, that is, the happy possibility of discovering a complete system which unites ancient and modern; its duty is to acknowledge ancient institutions as necessary, and subsequent useful practices as a natural development and progress in perfection of ancient institutions. However, this period of three generations is brief; it concerns only those upheavals (such as the recent revolutions in Europe) which spring from rational principles within Christianity. The theory is not applicable to political revolutions dependent upon brute instinct, or upon devastation caused by barbarians, or upon universal degradation (which can never be the case with Christianity).

85. I said that the second reason why the first institutions gradually lose their importance in public opinion is *the multiplicity of accidental institutions* which arise after them. In fact, whenever new institutions are established, people inevitably devote some attention to them. And the more rapidly they are instituted, the more people's attention (which is very limited), is distracted from substantial institutions.

86. This teaching provides an explanation for the duration of certain barbaric States. The Chinese, Tartars and Turks — and all nations denominated *static* because they show no signs of development and add no new accidental institutions to their ancient, substantial institutions — last for a long time because of their preoccupation with what gave and gives them existence; they are not distracted by accessories. If these commonalties did

[37] *Discorsi sulla prima Deca di T. Livio*, bk. 3, c. 16.

establish new institutions, as we do, they would crumble irreparably.

87. Many important corollaries flow from this. Here we will indicate only the following political maxims which are derived from the principles we have posited:

1. Every new, useless institution is harmful because it drains energy from the ancient institutions.
2. Every novel, accidental institution essentially brings some harm in its wake. It should not be undertaken, therefore, until political acumen shows that its utility will outweigh the damage it inflicts.
3. The best institutions will always be those which bond better with the ancient, substantial institutions, and thus harmonise with them.
4. It is indispensable for government to revive or reinforce by extensive education the memory of the intimate reason for fundamental political institutions.

CHAPTER 12

Substance and accident in social life: the struggle between two summary forces: the single aim of politics

88. So far we have explained in general the rule that society, if it wishes to continue and flourish, must possess a tendency drawing it unceasingly to consolidate its own being. It must not preoccupy itself with merely ornamental accessories which, if unimpeded, will indeed follow of their own accord as effects of vigorous, secure life in society. However, we have not yet explained the nature of this *being*, this *life* of society and this *substance*.

89. At this point a new, profound investigation must be undertaken. Anyone wishing to undertake it *ex professo* would find he had entered through the broad gate into the immense field of political science. This, however, is not what we intend. Our sole desire in this little work is to emphasise the importance of what appears to us as the first of all rules affecting the science of government in societies. Nevertheless we shall indicate at least one path which could help others to arrive at the secrets this important investigation has to unfold.

First we have to realise that human societies (similar in this respect to the bodies which make up the universe) are never static, but in continual movement with a constant change of state.

90. We can now determine two *limits*, that is, two extreme states which societies are forever approaching through their movement. These limits are the state of *maximum imperfection* in which society can be conceived, and the state of *maximum perfection*. We must also realise that every society moves between these two states in such a way that it tends in its motion sometimes towards the upper and sometimes toward the lower limit of perfection. These limits are never actually reached, however, despite proximity to them. On the one hand, supreme

perfection is never attained in human affairs; on the other, any society which could attain supreme imperfection would in fact have ceased to exist long before.

In the light of this never-ending change of generations, talents, humour, customs and proportion between things, it does appear, generally speaking, that two *summary forces* exist corresponding to the two *summary tendencies* or movements in society, one of which urges towards perfection, while the other gravitates towards imperfection. These forces, similar to the centrifugal and centripetal motions which control the tangential movements of stars, are the causes of all movement in the social universe, and form the two complex means with which in his wisdom the political theorist can, if he succeeds in grasping them, govern this universe.

91. We now need to consider more carefully the nature of what we have called *summary forces*.

Many particular forces act in human societies, and many causes produce effects. Part of these effects make perfect, part of them worsen and corrupt human beings and society. It is impossible to avoid this struggle between the mixture of good and evil agencies in any human society whatsoever; one cannot be found without the other. The sum of all favourable causes conspiring to bring about progress in the perfection of human beings and society, and the sum of all causes setting an obstacle to such perfection or destruction, are the two summary forces of which we are speaking.

92. Clearly, therefore, the state of society tends towards greater prosperity in so far as the first summary force prevails. Consequently, the whole art of government must have as its final aim, the intention of 'increasing as far as possible the first force, and decreasing the second'. We can affirm in general, without fear of error, that the *essential* scope of political dispositions is the prevalence of the first cause.

CHAPTER 13

Elements of the *two summary forces* which move society: the practical problems of political science

93. If we want to consider the separate complexes of the particular forces which taken together form the summary force moving society, we shall see that three parts have to be distinguished:

1. The *human spirit*, the source, in the last analysis, of the action through which anyone can work for the advantage or disadvantage of society. What I call 'collective unity', which gives existence to society itself, exists only in the human spirit.

2. *Things* which human beings find desirable (wealth, power, and so on) and their contraries. These are the matter which, informed by the energy of the human spirit, becomes an instrument of force.

3. The *object* of the force, that is, the social organism and ensemble over which every force finally exercises its operation.

In all three parts, we have to distinguish the essential from the accidental if we are to achieve our purpose.

94. Let us begin with the spirit, and consider it first in the individual. 'I succeeded because I really wanted to.' This was Napoleon's way of expressing the means by which resolute people have always brought about great changes in human affairs. The principal force behind great people[38] drives them to

[38] The following passages express vividly the character of the man whom, as we saw, found a great and feared empire. P. 2: 'I succeeded in what I undertook because I WANTED TO.' — 'For me, the world has always existed in FACT, not by RIGHT.' — p. 6: 'I studied war not on paper, but on the ground. I was under fire for the first time in a little confrontation with riflemen on the face of Mont-Genèvre. — It seemed clear to me that neither side had any intention of achieving a conclusion as a result of the shooting. They fired because their conscience told them to do so; it was simply what was expected of them in combat. This COMPLETE ABSENCE OF ANY OBJECT depressed me, etc.' — p. 7. 'I have given an account of my first experience under fire — it was this which initiated me into the secret of war. I realised

keep the end firmly in view, and energetically desire it. Insignificant people have no end in their activity, or confuse the end with the means, giving equal importance to both.

95. As society is a collective body, so it possesses a collective spirit. If we bring together on the one hand all the energy with which people composing society desire its existence and power, and on the other hand all the energy of wills inimical to the existence and power of society, we have two collective or social wills. One is 'positively favourable', the other 'positively contrary' to the existence of society.

96. If the stupidity or indolence of members of a society deprives them of all energy of will relative to social existence (as in the case described above when society has reached a stage when the immediate object of the masses is no longer social, but private — a period when the only stimulus to action is selfishness) we maintain that society has only a negative will, that is, it lacks the will which is its first and deepest vital force.

97. The existence of society is assured if *positive*, *favourable* will prevails within it. If *positive, contrary* will prevails, society no longer wishes to exist in fact, and is bound to fall. If no social will is present, society exists only accidentally, that is, it does not exist as a result of any force it receives from the spirit of its members, but solely as a result of the material solidity of its constitution — in other words, through its inertia. It stands like a stiffened corpse ready to fall at the first blow.

that it was easier than one thought to defeat the enemy, and that the great art consists in unhesitating action, and above all in attempting only decisive movements. This is the way to raise soldiers' morale.' — p. 9. 'Perhaps I was the only person in the army with some end in view; but my desire was to make this the end of everything. — I busied myself only in examining the enemy's position and our own. I compared his moral means and ours. I saw that we had them all, and he had nothing. His expedition was a feeble brainwave, a disaster he should have foreseen; and there is nothing more debilitating than staring defeat in the face.' — p. 40. 'We needed MORE THAN A HALF of Europe if the balance were to fall on our side. I was unable to provide myself with such a weight except by virtue of the law favouring the strongest, the only law to make inroads amongst the nations. Necessity demanded that I become the strongest. — I never had any choice about the decisions I had to take; events always dictated them. Danger was never far away.' — p. 66. 'My ambition never consisted in taking a few square miles of territory, but in making my cause triumph' (MS written at St. Helena).

98. A collective, favourable will is essential, therefore, for society. In other words, the will resulting from all individual wills must actually want whatever forms the existence and internal power of society, rather than the contrary. This is the first problem facing political theorists.

99. *Things*, or beings which form the matter or instrument used by the human spirit for the advantage or disadvantage of society are indifferent considered in themselves. Nevertheless, they exercise great pressure on human beings, despite the free activity of the human spirit which they do not always direct but certainly draw in one direction rather than another.

100. Although free will is not destroyed by attractions exercised on it, we have to bear in mind (when forming a judgment about the probability of human actions) that we have no other basis for our calculation. We must believe it more probable, therefore, that human beings will do whatever action results from greater pressure from their motives rather than omit that action or do something else. Moreover, a merely probable judgment about the actions of an individual becomes more or less certain relative to actions done by a multitude. If the entire population of a nation has strong motives for doing rather than omitting an action, we have to believe it almost morally certain that the majority will agree to do it, even though some individuals, by virtue of the energy of their free will, do not carry it out. The wise political theorist will, therefore, be able to foresee with great accuracy what will occur in a nation. This is the whole foundation and process of *political foresight*.

101. The objects used by the activity of the human spirit for good or evil in a society are *ownership* and *rights* and, more generally, everything that human beings can truly, or as a matter of opinion, look upon as good or evil, as desirable or to be feared. Because of this, the human spirit possesses a twofold relationship with these objects which, although indifferent when considered in themselves, can contribute to the good or evil of society.

102. The first relationship, as we have said, consists in the dominion the spirit has over these objects. Political theory, accompanied no doubt by moral science, has the obligation of teaching how these objects are to be employed to benefit rather than harm society.

103. The second relationship consists in the influence exercised over the human spirit by these same benefits (they do not force people to act, but according to their quantity and position persuade them to move in one direction rather than another). The second obligation of political science, therefore, is to deal with these objects and resolve the following problem: 'How can we find in society the best quantity and placement of objects which the human spirit considers good or bad for moving the will of human beings so that all work together for the existence and vigorous life of society?' This problem is more strictly political than the difficulty already discussed, which investigates the way in which the spirit of the members of society is educated to direct them socially. The first problem cannot be separated from ethics; the second deals with external facts only and with forces which, although they act on the spirit, are considered without reference to its free energy for the sake of reflecting mainly on the spirit's passivity.

104. Finally, the *object* of these wills, as they work together either spontaneously or moved and strengthened by external means, is social cohesion or management. At this point, the philosopher of politics has a third problem to solve: 'In the light of all unchangeable circumstances, especially natural circumstances, what kind of social management can give a more vital, enduring subsistence to society?'

105. Let us sum up. After the contrasting *wills* of the social members have confronted and mutually destroyed one another, a single will has to survive in favour of society itself. And precisely because it survives, it can be called 'the will of the social body'.

106. After the destruction of individual contrary actions, things which human beings consider good or bad, and hence influence the will and actions of the social body, must all act on this social will with their surviving activity so as to incline it in favour of society and render it suitable to operate with external effect.

107. Finally, those things which, through the energy of the spirit, exercise activity over the social body and mediate between the spirit of the individual and society, should operate favourably rather than unfavourably the existence of society. In

other words, they should improve, not worsen the *constitution* of the State.

CHAPTER 14

Three exclusive and therefore defective political systems: true political theory takes account of all elements

108. The three summary forces we have distinguished in the preceding chapter gave rise to three political systems, or rather to three ways of dealing with political science.

Many authors focused their whole attention on the importance to the social body of what we call a *positive, favourable will.* As a result they were principally engaged in showing how to direct public opinion. All *political moralists* of any kind belong to this group.

Others, who did not give too much direct importance to the strength of opinion, paid exclusive attention to everything that was external to human beings. These authors were principally anxious to deal with wealth and industry. They form the group known as *political economists*.

Finally, others, who considered *opinion* and *external goods* merely as accessories to political science, devoted themselves to the examination of the organism itself of the social machine, to the balance of powers which form it, and to the internal and external energy that results from this varying composition. These people are *political theorists in the strict sense*.

109. But from what we have said it is not difficult to understand that social science will never be complete as long as writers fix their biased, incorrect attention on only one of these three parts without considering the other two, or deal with the three parts as entirely separate without examining their relationships and factual unity.

110. Let us imagine that a government decides to take a certain step. Before doing this, it has to know if its decision will be opportune relative to the change it will induce in public spirit. In order to understand this, what has the government to consider?

111. It will certainly not be enough for the government, if it is wise, to know that the new disposition will better the spirit of a certain number or class of people. This would not enable the government to conclude that the step was truly useful. On the other hand, knowledge that the proposal would worsen the spirit of a certain number or class of people, should not be sufficient to dissuade it from action. The question has to be presented in another way if a well-advised judgment is to result. Thus we have to ask if, in taking the step under consideration, the government can make a probable calculation about the final good or bad effect of the favourable and unfavourable impressions that could be made on different spirits. In other words, will the public spirit grow better or worse, all things being considered? Moreover, if the effect on the spirit composing the society is bad rather than good, we still have to ask if the new arrangement is necessary to remove a greater evil. That is, if the step and its resultant disadvantage were avoided, would some even greater evil be expected?

112. Every question of political theory, therefore, is complicated and superior to normal forces. We are not asking about any particular good or evil, but about calculating a general good or evil. This explains the rashness of so many private judgments, as well as the unreality of almost all complaints springing from particular interests.

113. In the same way, it will never be possible to establish in political theory any general or *a priori* maxim as an answer to the question: 'Must a government make use of severity and terror in dealing with certain kinds of criminals?' Such terror may be useful in particular cases but harmful on a general level, or useful in general and harmful in particular according to the extent of depravity, crudity or culture in a given nation. And there are many other actual circumstances which are not considered by the question in the abstract.

The same can be said about other means which influence spirits. The opportuneness of these means can only be judged on the basis of knowledge of the *real* state of a nation. This is the only possible solid foundation on which to calculate the probable goodness or badness of the general effect, or the least bad effect which may be expected if such means are not taken.

114. If we apply the same reasoning to property, power and all

other external goods, we shall find that every political question in their regard must be reduced to a general calculation of the good or bad effect resulting from what we intend in their regard. Everything is reduced to knowing 'if the modification brought about in the distribution of wealth, or power, or any other good resulting from the new arrangement is of such a character that a general calculation shows it to be more useful than harmful.'

Every system, from that of an equitable distribution of property to that which attributes direct dominion over all property to the Sultan, can have its good and bad side. The defect of almost all writers of political science consists in demonstrating the benefits or defects of their imaginary system without bothering to strike a balance between good and bad. The aim at the end of the calculation would be to see which of the systems, in given circumstances, offers a more advantageous result; it is not a question of knowing which of the systems has no defects and contains every benefit.

115. *Perfectionism*, the system which believes in the possibility of perfection in human affairs and sacrifices present benefits for some imagined future perfection, is an effect of ignorance. It consists in overweening prejudice that prompts too favourable a judgment about human nature which it examines on the basis of pure hypothesis, of a postulate that cannot be granted, and with absolute lack of reflection on the natural limits of things.

Elsewhere I spoke about the great principle *of the limitation of things*, and I showed that THERE IS SOME GOOD WHOSE EXISTENCE WOULD BE ALTOGETHER IMPOSSIBLE WITHOUT THE EXISTENCE OF SOME EVIL.[39] Divine Providence itself, although most wise and powerful, is necessitated by this eternal, ontological principle. I mean that it is bound to calculate the total effect of what is good and what is bad, and permit the latter when it draws in its wake greater good. In the same way, it is obliged to produce amongst every possible good only that which does not occasion greater evil or impede greater good.

Granted, therefore, the unshakeable principle 'that occasionally the existence of some good *necessarily* impedes the existence

[39] *Saggio sulla divina Provvidenza nel governo de' beni e de' mali temporali*, included in the *Opuscoli Filosofici*, vol. 1, p. 117, Milan, 1827.

of a greater good, and that the existence of some good is often connected with the existence of certain evils, just as the existence of some evil is connected with what is certainly good, it is clear that all human wisdom in government can only be based on the imitation of the wisdom of the One who from heaven rules the entire universe. Human wisdom can only aim at obtaining the greatest *final* good effect, that is, the total good, as a result of calculating all the good and evil that serve as indispensable co-causes of the effect producing the greatest good. If we now express the benefits and disadvantages as respectively numerator and denominator, we shall see that government expertise does not consist solely in increasing the number of benefits or decreasing the disadvantages, but in ensuring that while benefits increase, disadvantages do not increase even further. Similarly, steps have to be taken to ensure that excessive disadvantages do not naturally diminish benefits to the detriment of the whole. In other words, the value of the resulting fraction must go up rather than down.[40]

116. What has been said about public spirit and about the quantity and distribution of external means can also be said 1. about the different modes of existence of social organism and management, and, 2. about their different parts, which are finally the objects on which the action of the two preceding forces focuses.

117. All foresight consists in arranging matters so that the endeavour to better some part of this organism or social cohesion does not result in damage to another, more essential part. In a word, we need to look for the general good of the whole organisation without being excessively partial to one of its parts.

118. However, even this is not sufficient. What we have said about each of these three systems of powers, that is, *public spirit*, *exterior benefits* and *social cohesion*, has to be repeated about all

[40] The thought I am trying to express will be more precise for those with some knowledge of mathematics if the benefits and disadvantages are expressed as two unknowns whose relationship is determined by any mutual function. The formula, $f(x,y) = o$, where x stands for something good, y for something disadvantageous, contains all possible values for x and y, and represents every possible relationship between these two quantities. As a result, it contains all laws about their relative increase and decrease.

three taken together. They are like three wheels on which revolve human social well-being. One influences another; one slows down or speeds up, collides with or helps another. None of them is so independent that it is free to act without reference to the damage it may cause the other two, if indeed it desires the harmony and the general welfare of the whole. In a word, the state and movement of each of the three wheels must accord with that of the other two, even if it loses something of its own action. And indeed we have seen more than once that excessive physical prosperity in a nation has caused its corruption and destruction. The notion that only some particular benefit in a nation need be considered, without reference to the rest, is fallacious in the extreme.

119. We conclude: the rule about substance and accident is transformed here into the rule which prescribes that wise governments should have a comprehensive vision which 'keeps in view the good of the whole, not simply that of a part.'

CHAPTER 15

The one formula to which every political problem is reduced: the necessity of statistics, and the ruling principle for their compilation

120. One consequence of our observations is that the science of government is seen simply as an unending problem about balance. The aim always is to discover the maximum good resulting from a mixture of good and ill as they increase and decrease according to certain laws.

121. Such a calculation cannot be made, however, until all the terms composing it have been known. It is highly desirable, therefore, that writers on politics should focus their precise attention on the moral, intellectual and physical state of peoples; high-flown declarations and vague, incomplete considerations are out of place. A special effort should be made to produce exact tables of the *proportions* of nations' physical goods as a whole and separately, of their mutual interaction, of their action in all that regards social life as a whole, and of the *physical symptoms* of the intellectual state and moral conditions of nations. This should be the *ruling principle* in the formation of truly political or, as Romagnosi would call them, civil statistics. It is clear, however, that statistics which aim at a complex calculation of all political forces for the sake of discovering the degree of social life or the true internal power constituting the subsistence of society will be altogether different from a simple 'economic description of nations' [*App.*, no.2], which statistics as a rule have presented until now.

122. It would also be desirable to reject as useless and dangerous any book whatsoever on political theory which did not reduce the question it dealt with to the general problem we have described.

123. Authors should be free to offer particular solutions to the problem, but at the same time be bound by the required form. If propositions are well set out, writers' weaknesses and so-

phistry are immediately obvious. People are deceived only by declamations and diatribes founded on vague ideas, and by fragmentary political questions unaccompanied by any projected and executed calculation of all the factors involved.

124. Such a calculation supposes society to be like a large, irregular body of which we have to find the centre of gravity, that is, the point where all the forces, after having partially destroyed one another, bring to bear their associated action and ensure that this centre does not fall outside the base.

125. But finding this centre of gravity and making this complicated calculation for the sake of discovering the prevailing residual force is either neglected, or carried out vainly or erroneously. This explains why theory so often contradicts actual experience. The *fact* of experience is the result of the simultaneous action of all the real forces, which may take different directions; it is finally the result of all that exists and operates in nature. *Theory*, on the other hand, is only the product of the often incomplete, fragmentary and accidental ideas that revolve almost by chance in the human mind. Nothing acts separately in fact; each part is connected with the whole. The mind, however, easily loses sight of one or other or many of these forces, and errs in its final calculation.

126. Our conclusion is obvious. A political teaching is not to be rejected simply because some defect is found in it, nor accepted because it contains some benefit. It is necessary to compare one teaching with all others to see if, in practice, the defect is perhaps the least possible deficiency, or if the benefit is mixed with much greater evils. We ought not condemn certain institutions as soon as they show some weak or defective side; we have to see rather if those defects are necessary.

It is clear, therefore, that the rules 'about existence and embellishment', 'about essence and accident' and finally 'about the whole and the part' are the same maxim expressed in different ways. It is the maxim found in many sayings or proverbs, such as: 'Divide and conquer', or 'Small things grow in harmony', and so on.

CHAPTER 16

The substantial form of society changes position; the law governing this change

127. What has been said so far seems clear and certain. In fact, it is not difficult to understand how the vigour of a State has to be found by making a calculation of all the forces which in their ultimate associated effect either come together to strengthen or destroy it, or cancel one another out in a collision of equal forces which leave the State extremely weak. Nor is it difficult to convince oneself that the supreme rule of government consists in increasing the total effect of all the contributing forces, in so far as this effect is favourable to social existence.

128. The difficulty lies in carrying out this complicated calculation in which the individual forces, many of which act quietly and secretly and thus escape the observation of even the wisest people, have first to be accurately assessed, then associated and finally evaluated from the point of view of the results of their various junctures.

129. A new investigation is now required, which would be of great assistance to such an important calculation. We have to enquire whether in the different states of a society there is some special force which prevails over others in such a way that taking account of it would be sufficient to save the society, even at the cost of neglecting other forces and considering them infinitely small compared with the prevalent force. We would then go on to consider whether such a force (which would consequently be the substance of society) would always be the same or whether it would, so to speak, change its position as society itself changed its state.

As everyone will see, this is a very serious question, requiring prolonged observation, accurate study of different human societies and great acumen.

130. It is from a calculation based on the facts of history that we should draw a demonstration of the following truth: 'In

different states of society there has been a prevalent force which has undergone variations in position as it has passed from one social element to another.' We should also show by means of facts 'the order in which the different social elements successively containing the prevalent force follow one another.' Then, by tracing the order of these elements as each in turn prevails, we should be able to establish one of the great laws of social movement which determine the series of different, progressive states reached by society when its movement is considered from this point of view.

131. Such an investigation cannot even be attempted in an essay as brief as this where we intend to touch only in passing what concerns the general question 'of the summary cause of the downfall and stability of societies'. Nevertheless, we shall offer some hints about this new problem.

132. We shall consider how the prevalent force changes position in the successive movements of Christian civil societies. What I am going to say will also illustrate what was affirmed when I maintained that Christian societies would never perish totally, but simply undergo upheavals and more or less serious afflictions from which, when these were overcome, such societies would emerge sounder and healthier than before. This usually occurs, I said, in the course of three generations. What I shall say now will prove in addition the constant progress made in Christian societies.

133. History has never perhaps provided a case in which civil society in Europe was subject to such violent pressure as in the last century. Any ancient society would have perished under such an assault.

134. The deepest foundations of social life were targeted. The 18th century was a century of material teachings; the branches of knowledge concerning the spirit were abandoned, calumniated and almost annihilated as the century applied itself exclusively to material development. Everything connected with quantity was the object of incredibly intense study; mathematics, the mechanical arts and everything concerned with the professions, commerce and industry certainly made swift and marvellous progress. But this is only an *accident* relative to peoples' happiness. Matter is subject to division; the spirit on the contrary reduces all things to unity, in which alone resides

the force which constitutes true, social power. Matter is an external, superficial object; the spirit is an internal, fundamental subject, the inner home of true satisfaction, under threat from external disquiet and need.

135. As a result, the century most developed in material, accidental knowledge was blinded to the principles and elements of civil life; those responsible for defending society from assault committed the grossest errors. Supremely anxious about accidents, they gave no thought to substance; they neglected the whole for the part.

136. Only France, as the aggressor, gave momentary signs of real energy as she attacked all the European States (and all their institutions) which, having lost sight of the reasons for their foundation, were scarcely able to defend themselves. Only very late in the day did they realise that the struggle was not about the loss of useless, out-dated practices, but about the loss of everything, existence included. This explains why the heads of government were so slow to act and so disunited in face of a nation which laid assault to everything ancient. Ignoring the danger to their existence, they preferred to keep their sight on commerce.[41] An acute writer notes:

> Ximenes and Richelieu should have noted the revolution taking place within human spirits. But Europe's administrators, like their century, were preoccupied with factories, banks, embellishments, arts and roads; in other words, they paid more attention to *things* than to *human beings*, and saw in the French revolution simply a great lottery in which neighbouring States had everything to gain. The weak would gain without risking anything; the strong would gain in proportion to what they contributed.[42]

137. Nevertheless, when the crisis came and people began to

[41] In 1795, the Grand Duke of Tuscany, abandoning the cause common to the Italian Princes and the whole of Europe for fear of a temporary interruption to trade, sent Carletti to France to sue for peace. The people 'were intensely glad. This was especially true of the citizens of Liverno, where commerce was flourishing. They praised the wisdom of Grand Duke Ferdinand who, oblivious to the indignation of Europe, aimed at happiness for his subjects by gaining for them security and a quiet life' (Botta, *Ist. d'Ital.*, bk. 5).

[42] Bonald, *Discours politiques sur l'état actuel de l'Europe*, §1.

see the consequences of the overthrow of the ancient foundations, many awoke from what seemed a deep stupor. As we said, it is precisely when existence is in danger that many individuals rouse themselves in Christian nations to produce hidden intellectual and moral force capable of bridling the course of the multitudes. People begin to reflect and cease to lose themselves in the frivolous pursuit of accidentals. They look finally for a substantial force capable of sustaining society. But despite searching everywhere — in human beings, in things, in principles — they do not easily find it.

138. Let us see what has happened during the past forty years, and ask ourselves if this force has been found, and where.

The first thought that comes to mind — and it occurs almost invariably when the State needs reinforcing — is that of brute *force*. This is, in fact, the sole hope of aggressors who know only too well that 'innovators have to be well-armed, and that force rather than prayer is needed if their work is to succeed.'[43]

139. Society possessed individuals who thought seriously about the brute force possessed by society, and used it. But it was not enough. Human beings and things are sufficient for all those struggles in which *human beings* and *things* play their part without reference to *principles*. In other words, the world, as long as it finds itself in a certain state of undevelopment, takes no thought about changing its *principles*. Everyone, friends and enemies alike, accepts them without discussion and respects them. At moments like these, every battle is fought between human beings and between things. But circumstances change; principles themselves are drawn into the conflict. Everything is re-thought, everything called into doubt, as in the last century. At this point, it is vain to rely solely on human prudence or on the number of physical forces. No government can hope any longer to factually prevail with these means alone. The battle is no longer between these elements; a *force superior* to them both has entered the lists. This force, the force of *principles*, disposes both of *human beings* and *things* as it wishes. Principles sown in the mind govern human beings, and through them human af-

[43] Machiavelli, *Del Principe*, c. 6.

fairs. In this state, and we have seen it in our own days, a once *substantial* force becomes *accidental.*

140. Three moments have to be distinguished, therefore, in the vicissitudes which the world has undergone until now. First, the moment in which *physical force* alone almost came to dominate. Whoever prevailed through strength, or show of arms, endured.

Soon, a subtle kind of *prudence*, or astuteness, took the place of force, especially when wealth was brought into play.[44] A greater effect is produced by a lesser, well directed force than by greater force which lacks direction. In this state of affairs, physical force, which had now become accidental, was no longer the *greatest* power. Cleverness and ability of spirit became the greatest and the substantial power. *Things* had ceded to *human beings.*

141. Experience, however, soon showed that there was nothing more uncertain or weak than human prudence and individual astuteness. No one was so clever that another, cleverer person could not arise; and there was certainly no one who was incapable of failing in what he undertook. Moreover, nature's

[44] Signor Carlo Dupin, in his work *Forze produttive e commerciali della Francia*, offers as a sure criterion for estimating the capacity of nations the quantity and quality of their *productive and commercial forces.* This is partially true, that is, it is true for the second of the three steps we have distinguished in the history of States, when *wealth* prevails over *force*. We are now at the stage of human ingenuity and prudence, not of things. But Signor Dupin's criterion would not be valid if, for example, it were applied to the Romans in the finest hour of the republic, the first of the three steps when *force* prevails over *wealth.* Nor would it be valid if it were applied to the third step in which moral principles prevail (the point at which we would hope to have finally arrived). In passing, I would like to note here that each of the three stages I have distinguished (things, human beings, principles) has its own proper *statistics.* At the first step, the *governing principle* of statistics is the calculation of the prevalent force, that is, of the force consisting in physical *forces* (population, armed forces, and so on); at the second, the governing principle is found at a higher level where it calculates intellectual forces, especially the forces of *production* and *commerce*, in addition to physical forces. Finally, the statistics of the third and last step are raised to the dignity of moral statistics. Their *governing principle* is far more sublime and broad than those of the two preceding steps. Calculation is now made of all other forces in relationship to the force of the *principles* which move human beings and things. In these statistics everything is complete and unified. And these are the statistics which must be compiled in our days.

erratic distribution of the prudence and astuteness in which dominion over things existed, had to be an everlasting source of disturbance and change. This must have been especially clear after the development of common knowledge which gave everyone the opportunity of developing his own capacities and fighting his own corner. As a result, people recognised that the need for secure properties, small and great, was no longer satisfied by dependence upon the doubtful outcome of sheer cleverness which became so prevalent that perpetual lying and self-destruction took the place of any kind of solid conclusion. Hence the recognition of the happy need to agree finally about *moral principles*.

In this way, God gently guided human beings through the pressure of self-interest to bow before the *truth*. Indeed, all parties, even those dissatisfied with the quality of the right they have received, must admit the solemn fact that only in our days have we witnessed powerful rulers arrive at an agreement in which all declared that their confidence and individual glory rests solely upon the common principles of justice, faith and religion. The only harm religion suffered from its enemies was a unanimous judgment from the greatest monarchs of Europe who proclaimed it the sole protectrix of the States and the unique source of public happiness![45]

[45] A recent author commented as follows: 'Besides the popular opposition which sovereigns had to face at home, the events of the past ten years have revealed the deficiencies inherent in coalitions and their insufficiency in such extraordinary circumstances. Cabinets which supported the ancient right of nations in Europe retained their old habits also. For them, the perfection of diplomacy consisted in astuteness; they would have been ashamed not to have had devious secrets and not to have had in view ends more distant than those towards which they openly worked. The "balance of power" system meant that States always needed to view one another with mutual suspicion. Trickery, carried out with the intention of hiding from other powers one's own ambitions of aggrandisement, was indeed innocent up to a certain point in a peaceful epoch, such as that which preceded the revolution; the matter in hand could not have been of great importance. But now, everything had changed, and it was still not possible to convince people that the question was not a matter of possessing more or less, but of losing everything. It was no longer sufficient to think of anything less than the common danger; only a truthful, disinterested and loyal policy could save European independence. The advantages gained by one of the allied powers excited the jealousy of the

142. Thus, the best Provider of all, who has fixed a law for all beings, has driven human beings towards the *truth*.

As we noted, three moments are well established in the progress made by things. If we think about the moments carefully, considering them as three levels of human advancement, or as three terms of a continuous series, it will not be difficult to imagine a fourth level or term towards which the state of humanity seems to advance ineluctably. I realise, of course, that not everyone will share my opinion, but nevertheless I believe it to be very probable and clear.

143. As human society moves forward from positing its foundation and guarantee first in *force*, then in *foresight*, and finally in the *principles* of justice and the Christian religion, it passes continuously from a weaker force to a stronger force, from a less true force to one more true, from an external to an internal force. My own firm belief, therefore, is that we now have to move, within the same teaching on justice, from an external, incomplete *right* to a perfect right, that is, from *right* to *morality* taken in its broadest sense. We have to place the supreme social force in the unlimited practice of VIRTUE, and finally recover from within Christianity its most solid, complete and intimate factor, in order to establish the tranquillity and well-being of nations. And there is no doubt that this factor is Catholicism.

In the end, only Catholicism will be found to stand firm; only Catholicism, a truly complete religion with followers who are simultaneously fully enlightened and sincere, possesses solidity and an absolute capacity. From then on, there will be no question of seeking something more solid, but of rendering Catholicism itself ever purer in people's minds, ever deeper in their hearts and ever more effective in practice. This will be the final work of perfect political theory.

If these things are considered carefully, it will not be difficult to see what is required today from those who govern. It seems to me certain that people in power will undoubtedly perish if they inadvertently oppose this natural movement of human affairs, or refuse to take refuge in the shelter to which they are

others; the damage suffered by one in particular was looked at with indifference and sometimes with satisfaction by its rivals. Rapprochement was accompanied by distrust, and separation by irritation' (*Del sistema continentale*).

driven by ineluctable, joyous necessity. Our present condition requires that the on-going struggle for existence should make no one anxious about losing some partial prerogative or external splendour. Everyone must learn to judge sagely the stupid or even blameworthy counsels of those who flatter human passions with the aim of persuading others to fight over tiny, adventitious, uncertain or pretended rights instead of maintaining their own greater, fundamental rights.[46]

[46] There are people profoundly aware of the present state of things who see in our modern tranquillity an untrustworthy calm that presages some disastrous storm. Napoleon was certainly amongst these prophets of woe. His feelings are expressed in *Pensées philosophiques d'un ci devant philosophe souverain* even though the words may not be his. Less exaggerated, but more authoritative are the words of Leo XII: 'Beloved children, it has always been necessary, but is now more necessary than ever, to return to the heart, to bring forth worthy fruits of penance, and TO FLEE THE WRATH THAT IS TO COME. Present evils forcefully persuade us that worse could befall unless we take heed and truly return to sounder ways. Even now his hand is extended'. And we should note that amongst the sovereigns of Europe only Pius VI foresaw and proclaimed in time the imminent evils. He was neither heard nor believed, and unbelievers harvested the whirlwind.

CHAPTER 17

Conclusion

144. It is now time to conclude our little treatise. Let me repeat: the government of divine Providence itself follows the norm we have considered as the supreme principle of human government, that is, substance is to be firmly maintained whatever happens to accidents.

In order to grasp this, we have to search deep within the divine economy relative to the human race; we have to study the history of the kingdom of God on earth, and of the continuous, ferocious battles that kingdom has to sustain.

145. If we do this, we shall uncover the foundation of the two great classes into which holy Scripture divides mankind, the *children of light* and the *children of darkness*. The former cling to the *truth*, that is, to the *light*; the latter adhere to *falsity*, that is, to *darkness*. God takes his place at the head of the children of light, reserving for himself and those who belong to him the knowledge of *beings per se*, and dominion over them. He leaves to his opponents, who want to set up their own power against his might, knowledge of *beings per accidens* and, to a certain extent, power to dominate them. He holds firmly to substance, and abandons accidents to his enemies; he enfolds knowledge, and leaves sophistry to others; he holds the final outcome in his hands while his opponents preen themselves on their incomplete success; to him the *effect*, to his adversaries, only the *hope* of the effect.

146. These are the two great teachings, the two great loves, the two powers, the two glories. One is founded on what is necessary and indestructible; the other on what is accidental and changeable, the source of perpetual illusion, unending deceit, continual uncertainty, interminable destruction. These are the two hinges of the whole of God's system, upon which revolves the real, intellectual and moral universe. In the whole universe there are only two entities: one ministering supreme mercy; the

other, supreme justice. This divine intention in creating, preserving and governing things is visible everywhere; it demonstrates and teaches the nature of the first principle of every government.

147. This is a *cosmic* law, a law of both the moral and physical world. It is the law that renders indestructible the element of matter, despite all the changes of form that matter undergoes from mechanical and chemical means; it is the law ensuring that one thing is born immediately from the corruption of another while the base never perishes; it is the law that tempers the boldness of mankind, that puts a fixed term to the tempestuous ocean of humanity; it is the law that preserves everything which shares in the universal order, while all attempts at disturbing the order fail; it is the law that confirms the saying of a sublime thinker: 'The principles of Christianity are simply the divinised laws of the world.'[47]

[47] De Maistre, *Soirées de Saint-Pétersbourg*, IX Entretien.

Appendix

1. (35)

I would like to make other observations about Romagnosi's *Memoria*, to which I have already referred.

1. Unlike Romagnosi, we must be careful not to confuse two totally distinct questions. The first is a universal but merely theoretical question: 'Is it true that population, of its nature, grows in geometrical progression, but that the means of subsistence can grow only in arithmetical progression, and even this in a limited way? According to the physical law governing growth, does population really grow more rapidly than the means of subsistence? Consequently, is it true that, wherever moral causes do not curb procreation, the population will eventually exceed the means of subsistence and succumb to misery?' This is the first question. The second, a purely factual question, asks: 'Is it true that the population of this country at the moment exceeds the means of subsistence?' The answer to the first question must certainly be affirmative. In the case of the second, all the facts must be carefully assembled and a decision made in accordance with them. But Romagnosi confuses the two questions by applying to the first arguments which are valid only for the second.

2. In addition, he says: 'If Malthus and his school show me that the social commandment of the divine Kingdom and its justice has taken effect there (in Ireland and England), we can indeed discuss whether the sufferings of so many unfortunate people should be ended.' Frankly, these words are ill-considered and out of place.

No matter how oppressive the rich may be, or how unfairly possessions divided, do we have to wait until the rich are more sympathetic and possessions better shared on earth before we try to remedy the sufferings of the poor? It is utterly pointless to declaim against the rich and the estate owners. What we need to know, granted that at the moment no one has the power to abolish poverty, is whether the number of poor is excessive.

My opinion is this: there are poor people precisely because the kingdom of God is not yet perfect and universal on earth. And while the poor are among us, we must think of alleviating, if not ending, their suffering. The problem is how to do all this with justice and real charity.

2. (121).

This [an economic description of nations] is Gioia's definition of statistics (*Filosofia della statistica*, t. 1, *Discorso elementare*). Romagnosi has a much higher concept of statistics, at least as regards *method*. But relative to *evaluating* the elements necessarily present in statistics, an accurate criterion cannot be determined by any author who, basing himself on the doctrine of sensist and utilitarian philosophers, declares that 'the apex of the true civilization of human associations consists in free and guaranteed *economic* competition' (*Sulla crescente popolazione*, *Memoria* of G. D. Romagnosi, Milan, 1830). Whatever importance is given to economic matters, it will never be true that the apex of human associations consists in *economy*. Romagnosi's merit lies indisputably in his *method*, not in his *content*. The value of his ideas about statistical method is that he takes a more complex view than his predecessors, and feels the need to accept and take account of all elements. His description of the political power of a State confirms this. We can easily see that he makes great efforts to assemble all the elements of this power: 'The political power of a State consists in the degree of *culture*, *patriotism* and *population* in a country adapted to communal living, and in the union of the means originating from these causes. This must naturally give birth to the common security and satisfaction of a people living in political society' (*Questioni sull'ordinamento delle statistiche*, Question 6). But despite his effort to detail what he has to say, the three words *culture*, *patriotism* and *population* are clearly too vague to indicate exactly the elements of a nation's internal power. Not every *culture* makes a nation stronger; *patriotism* must be enlightened; the *population* must be not only proportionate to the means of subsistence but uniform and united. Thus the determined *degree* of the three things mentioned by Romagnosi is not sufficient to form a satisfying, secure community. In addition to the *degree*, account must be taken of the *quality* of things. Furthermore, granted the common security and satisfaction of the people, internal power will vary according to the degree of strength of the organism, the degree of wealth and its disposability by the government, the ability of outstanding people in the nation, and many other circumstances. Finally, Romagnosi entirely omits the supreme force of moral principles, which is not always in proportion to culture, patriotism and population. These principles are at times fresh and active in people's minds; at other times sluggish and ineffective. However, as Romagnosi himself says so well, it is always true that 'this power must be considered as a solid, single product of all the contributing, associated causes' (*ibid.*).

Index of Persons

Numbers in roman indicate paragraphs or, where stated, the appendix (app.); numbers in italic indicate footnotes. Bracketed numbers refer to the Preface.

General Index

Numbers in roman indicate paragraphs or, where stated, the appendix (app.); numbers in italic indicate footnotes. Bracketed numbers refer to the Preface.